PEACE

===== AND =====

GOOD

ORDER

The Case for
Indigenous Justice
in Canada

HAROLD R. JOHNSON

McCLELLAND & STEWART

McClelland & Stewart and colophon are registered trademarks of
Penguin Random House Canada Limited.

Library and Archives Canada Cataloguing in Publication data is
available upon request

ISBN: 978-0-7710-4872-2
ebook ISBN: 978-0-7710-4873-9

Book design by Leah Springate
Typeset in New Caledonia LT Std by M&S, Toronto
Printed and bound in the USA

McClelland & Stewart,
a division of Penguin Random House Canada Limited,
a Penguin Random House Company
www.penguinrandomhouse.ca

2   3   4   5   23   22   21   20   19

To the next seven generations.

CONTENTS

※

OPENING ARGUMENT

❖

THE CASE AGAINST CANADIAN JUSTICE

Late in the evening on February 9, 2018, I heard the decision in the Gerald Stanley trial announced on the radio. An all-white jury had found Stanley not guilty of shooting and killing Colten Boushie, a twenty-two-year-old Cree man from the Red Pheasant First Nation. On August 9, 2016, Boushie and four of his friends—Kiora Wuttunee, Cassidy Cross-Whitstone, Eric Meechance and Belinda Jackson—had spent the day swimming. Cassidy Cross-Whitstone was driving their Ford Escape home when they hit a culvert and punctured a tire. They pulled into a farm belonging to Gerald Stanley, a fifty-six-year-old white man, and Cross-Whitstone and Meechance got out their vehicle.

They were confronted by Stanley and his son Sheldon, who believed the men intended to steal an ATV. Meechance and Cross-Whitstone jumped back into the Escape and tried to drive away, but veered into Gerald Stanley's car and crashed. While Sheldon Stanley ran toward the house, Gerald Stanley grabbed a semi-automatic handgun from his shed. When Stanley fired two warning shots, Cross-Whitstone and Meechance ran off, leaving Colten Boushie and the two women in the Escape. At trial, conflicting testimony was offered as to what happened next: Gerald Stanley testified that when he lunged into the Escape to take the keys from the ignition the gun went off accidentally, hitting Colten in the head. Belinda Jackson testified that the gun was fired intentionally. Twelve white jurors believed Mr. Stanley.

After twenty years as a lawyer, having worked first as defence counsel and then as a prosecutor in the high-crime communities of northern Saskatchewan, I experienced some vicarious trauma in response to the verdict. I shut off the radio and ignored all social media. I didn't want to be part of it. I wanted to hide in my cabin on my trapline with my wife, my writing and my dog team and pretend that I was not part of that world. It wasn't my file. I hadn't been hired by the accused or the family of the victim. I had retired, thankfully, and so hadn't been involved in the case in any way. I could tell myself it was none of my business, and no one had asked me to make it so.

The next morning I awoke to find a text message on my phone from a dear friend, a retired provincial court judge.

Harold,

I hope that you're fast asleep and that this text doesn't wake you. It's 12:38 a.m. I'm sitting at my kitchen table and I'm crying. I'm ashamed. I'm ashamed. After hearing the verdict in the Stanley case in North Battleford I'm ashamed. I'm ashamed of my Caucasian heritage. And I should have seen how stacked the system is against indigenous Canadians. I feel so ashamed, and I must be sorry for myself too because I want to cry.

The forbearance of the families who suffer this is more than I can understand right now.

I'm sorry to bother you with this, Harold. I just needed to tell somebody how sad I feel.

Later that day, my wife and I left our home in the boreal forest. We were heading more than four hundred kilometres south, down to Sweetgrass First Nation, near Colten's home, to attend a ceremony. As I drove,

I had lots of time to think about what my friend had said in our subsequent conversation. "The thing that discourages me so much is that I believe that in rural, farmland Saskatchewan, there are many that believe Stanley had the right to kill Colten Boushie."

My friend would know. After a career as a lawyer and then a judge in northern Saskatchewan, he retired to a ranch in the south, happy to be back where he grew up, close to family and horses. He heard all the things his farmer neighbours were saying. Coming together in local restaurants and other meeting places, they reinforced each other's dislike of Indigenous Peoples. When the majority of a community believes the stereotypes, and when the jury is selected from this pool, the acquittal of a white farmer in the shooting of an Indigenous man is all but guaranteed.

While we were crossing that desolate land, far from the nearest gas station or other facility with a washroom, my wife asked me to pull over, and she stipulated, "Not in a farmyard." I realized that this tough woman, who lives with me on a trapline, who regularly walks trails alone in the dark knowing there are wolves out there, whom I have never seen to be afraid of anything, was now afraid of farmers.

And if we believe Gerald Stanley, the farmers were afraid of her.

What do I know about fear? Not much. I know that if a dog is afraid, it is more likely to bite than a dog that is angry. I know that if a person is afraid for long enough, their fear turns into anger and their anger becomes hate. And I know that hate leads to suffering.

Shortly after the Stanley decision, the Indigenous street gangs in Saskatchewan informed First Nations leadership that they were armed and prepared to start shooting. All they needed was for someone to give them the okay. Our leadership told them to stand down. The Saskatchewan government, in an effort to garner votes, added fuel to the fire by issuing assault rifles to conservation officers and altering trespass laws to remove the assumption of free access to unoccupied lands. There is no reason to give conservation officers assault rifles other than to send a message that Saskatchewan is prepared to go to war with its Indigenous population. All that was needed in the province for a full-blown race war was one more incident, one more death, and for leadership on both sides to use the incident for their own political ends.

Indigenous Peoples across Canada were extremely upset by the Stanley decision. It seemed that Canadian justice cared more about the property rights of settlers than about the lives of Indigenous youth. Gerald Stanley had used deadly force to protect his property, and the law decided that was okay. Meanwhile, Indigenous Peoples were serving prison time at an ever-increasing rate.

The 2017/18 annual report of the federal Office of the Correctional Investigator stated:

> In the ten-year period between March 2009 and March 2018, the Indigenous inmate population increased by 42.8% compared with a less than 1% overall growth during the same period. As of March 31, 2018, Indigenous inmates represented 28% of the total federal in-custody population while comprising just 4.3% of the Canadian population. The situation continues to worsen for Indigenous women. Over the last ten years, the number of Indigenous federally sentenced women increased by 60%, growing from 168 in March 2009 to 270 in March 2018. At the end of the reporting period, 40% of incarcerated women in Canada were of Indigenous ancestry. These numbers are distressing.

The over-incarceration of Indigenous Peoples continues despite efforts to slow it down. In 1995, the Canadian government amended section 718.2(e) of the Criminal Code to require judges, upon sentencing Indigenous offenders, to consider their unique circumstances. Despite the change to legislation, though, the incarceration rate has continued to climb. The Supreme Court of Canada, in the Gladue decision in 1999, told judges they had to obey the Criminal Code and specifically told them which circumstances to consider, including the effects of the residential school system, family breakdown, dislocation, dispossession, poverty and poor living conditions. Yet still the incarceration rate climbed. The Supreme Court, in the Ipeelee decision in 2012, again told judges they had to obey the Criminal Code, and again nothing changed.

In the 1940s and '50s there were very few Indigenous people in prison. Disparities with regard to the incarceration of Indigenous men began only in the 1960s and have steadily widened since then. Incarceration rates of Indigenous women have begun to follow this same upward curve. The incarceration rates of children likewise continue to increase, with no end in sight. The incarceration rate of Indigenous Peoples in Saskatchewan is among the highest in the world.

The country with the highest overall incarceration rate is the United States, where more than 700 out of every 100,000 people are in custody. In Canada that rate is much lower. Here we incarcerate about 114 out of every 100,000. Compared with the rest of the world, we are average. England's incarceration rate is about

148 per 100,000 and Japan's is about 62 per 100,000. The rate in Saskatchewan is higher than the national and the global average. In this province we incarcerate about 207 out of every 100,000.

In 2015/16, Saskatchewan had an average of 1,812 people in custody on any given day. Of that number, 76 percent, or 1,378, were Indigenous. Indigenous Peoples in Saskatchewan represent 16.3 percent of the province's population. The incarceration rate among the Indigenous population in Saskatchewan is about 786 out of every 100,000, which is higher than the overall rate in the U.S.

Everyone is fully aware of the numbers. We all know that there are far too many Indigenous people in custody, and we've known for some time.

The 1996 Royal Commission on Aboriginal Peoples reported on incarceration rates in Saskatchewan. Between 1976 and 1993 Saskatchewan experienced a 54 percent increase in the number of people it incarcerated; Indigenous Peoples accounted for 77 percent of that increase.

And we know that incarceration makes things worse for people. In 2002, the Solicitor General of Canada investigated whether imprisonment reduced crime. A report that reviewed 117 studies involving roughly 442,000 offenders and their sentences concluded that harsher penalties not only did not reduce crime, but they increased the likelihood that offenders would commit crimes in the future. In Saskatchewan, the Commission on First Nations and Métis Peoples and Justice Reform reported in 2004: "Imprisonment will not reduce crime. This has been proven through research and the failure of Saskatchewan's 'get tough' practices. Saskatchewan incarcerates more youth per capita and still has the highest crime rate in Canada. Politicians, judges, and court system participants must provide accurate information to the public about the failure of imprisonment as an effective deterrent to crime."

Clearly, what we are doing is not working. Yet we continue doing it, on and on, making things worse.

When I returned from the ceremony in southern Saskatchewan, I called a few friends, and together we set up a fish derby to commemorate the signing of the 1889 Adhesion to Treaty 6. My great-grandfather James Ross had attended some of those treaty negotiations 130 years earlier, on February 11, 1889. Treaty 6 had been negoti-ated between Canada and the Plains Cree in 1876 and encompassed 120,000 square miles of primarily prairie land. The adhesion in 1889 between Canada and my people, the Woods Cree, added another 11,000 square miles of boreal forest to the treaty territory.

The Cree phrase *aski poko* was fundamental to the negotiations of this adhesion. Directly translated, *aski poko* means "land only." My ancestors were told that the Crown wanted the right to cut timber and mine minerals. When they asked about the fish, they were told that their fishing would not be interfered with. When they asked about the things that swam—the beaver and the muskrat—they were told that their trapping would not be interfered with. My great-grandfather and others at those negotiations believed that they had kept jurisdiction over the water and that all they gave up was the dry land, *aski poko*.

In accordance with these promises, James Ross refused to ever buy a hunting or fishing licence. His sons would purchase one for him and carry it on his behalf, but he insisted that he had not given up the right to live as he had before the treaty. Canada, he said, had no jurisdiction over him when it came to how he made his living from the territory.

Those 1889 negotiations occurred a few hundred metres from where I now live, at the north end of Montreal Lake. This site has been used by my ancestors for thousands of years. I find evidence of our history and connection to this place when the sands on the beach are shifted by rising and dropping water levels and shards from knapping arrowheads rise to the surface. When my ancestors negotiated Treaty 6, it was an agreement to share the wealth of this territory with the newcomers. All the wealth generated from this territory comes from the rights—to cut timber, to mine minerals, to build roads and villages and cities—received at treaty, and I would go so far as to argue that Canada's right to exist is a Treaty Right.

In Canada there is a widely held expectation that the law will be fair. Indigenous Peoples expect that when a white man kills an Indigenous person, he will be treated with the same sternness that has been applied to us. Law is fundamental to the relationship between Indigenous Peoples and settlers. But while we might *expect* fairness, our experience has been otherwise.

Everything that has been done to Indigenous Peoples has been legal. Law was used to deny us access to the natural resources within the territories we share with settlers. Law has been used to confine us to tiny plots that are economically unsustainable. Under the pass system, introduced by law in 1885 and not repealed until 1951, Indians needed the permission of the Indian agent to leave our reserves to visit neighbouring relatives or to go hunting or fishing or gathering, and the Indian agent relied upon the police to enforce his decisions to deny permission. Law gave huge tracts of our territory to foreign corporations to exploit the natural resources, depriving us of sacred sites, food sources, medicines and income. We were arrested if we entered into territory where our parents, grandparents and great-grandparents had lived, hunted, fished, trapped and gathered. When the Prince Albert National Park was created in 1927, it was the RCMP who came to tell my mother's family that the territory where they lived and found sustenance had become a park and they had to leave their houses and their gardens and the trails and the land and animals they were familiar with and move somewhere else.

Canadian law determined who we were. Under the terms of the Indian Act, if a First Nations woman married a non–First Nations man, she lost her status as an Indian. She and her children lost their right to hunt, fish and gather. If they were caught hunting or fishing, they frequently were arrested, charged, convicted and sentenced to jail—for the crime of feeding their families. I can remember when I was young and my mother's brother Ben was arrested and sent to jail for hunting. Not only did his immediate family suffer; the entire community suffered because Ben was an exceptional hunter who provided meat to a lot more people than just his wife and children. I was born in a small northern community of trappers and fishers to a Cree mother and a Forest-Finn Swede father. It was not until 2011 that the Indian Act was changed and Canadian law recognized me as an Indian.

Indigenous Peoples were not only the subject of laws that encircled and diminished us. We were also denied the ability to resist those laws. Any other Canadian citizen who was the subject of an unjust law could challenge that law in court. We could not. From 1927 until 1951, it was against the law for Indigenous people or communities to hire a lawyer, without the government's consent, to bring claims against the government to restore lands or rights taken away by that government.

Law has been used to compel us to surrender our children to residential schools, where horrors were inflicted upon them in an attempt to eradicate our culture and language. The police were instrumental in rounding up our children. (My mother attended a residential school for one year, in about 1930, and several of my cousins were sent in the 1970s and '80s. My siblings and I were spared that horror.)

Law was used again in the 1960s, when social workers, accompanied by police officers, removed Indigenous children from their homes on the pretext that they were not being cared for properly. After my father died, my mother was told that if she continued to take me and my siblings out of school to go to the trapline with her, the government would take her children away. In 1967, if you told an Indigenous woman with one year of schooling and six children at home that you were going to take her children away from her, she would do anything she was told. My mother surrendered her independence. She moved us to a larger community, where she was forced to go on welfare.

And law has been used to fill the jails with Indigenous men, women and children at rates that continue to rise. Not only are Indigenous people more likely to be sentenced to prison, but they are also subject to some of the most restrictive types of punishment, including segregation, high-security classifications and involuntary transfers.

To say that law and justice have failed Indigenous Peoples in Canada is a vast understatement. Law and justice appear to be the tools employed to continue the forced subjugation of an entire population.

Back in February 2018, we were too late to hold the derby on the adhesion's anniversary date, but we managed to hold the First Annual Our Treaty Fish Derby a couple of weeks later. The derby was endorsed by the Town of La Ronge, the Lac La Ronge Indian Band, the Village of Air Ronge and the Montreal Lake Cree Nation. A group of First Nations people and settlers came together to celebrate our treaty because it belongs to everyone and is the basis of the relationship between Indigenous Peoples and settlers. We came together and experienced each other as human beings on the land we share and learned not to be afraid of each other.

Then I began writing this book.

My retired judge friend had said that he was ashamed of his time involved in the justice system. I too feel this way about my time as both defence counsel and Crown prosecutor: ashamed that I didn't have the courage to stand up in the courtroom and shout, "Enough is enough!"

The last residential school in Canada closed in 1996, and in 2008, Prime Minister Stephen Harper apologized to residential school survivors. In 2017, Prime Minister Justin Trudeau apologized to the LGBTQ2 community for government policy from the 1950s to the early 1990s. In 2019, Prime Minister Trudeau again apologized, this time for the discriminatory way Inuit with tuberculosis were treated between 1940 and 1960. And someday in the future a prime minister of Canada is going to stand up and apologize for my participation in the over-incarceration of Indigenous Peoples.

This book is my act of taking responsibility for what I did, for my actions and inactions.

TESTIMONY

1

I fell into law by chance.

I NEVER WANTED to be a lawyer. I fell into law by chance.

I was born in a small northern community of trappers and fishers. I grew up believing I could be a trapper and fisherman because those were the stories I heard. I didn't know any lawyers. The first lawyer I ever spoke to was Alice Robert, who was hired by the United Steelworkers of America, the trade union I belonged to.

In 1991, I was working at the Key Lake uranium mine, in northern Saskatchewan, as a heavy equipment operator. There was a story going around, primarily among management but also among the workers, that if you operated a Cat or a haul truck, you were stupid. To prove I wasn't stupid, I quit the mines to go to university. I picked what I thought was the hardest course of study. I picked law not because I wanted to be a lawyer but to prove a point: Harold Johnson isn't stupid.

If you are Indigenous and you get a bachelor's degree in anything, people will say you didn't earn it. The school just gave it to you because you are an Indian. To prove no one gave me anything, I went to Harvard and got a master's degree in law.

It took five years, from when I left the mines with less than a grade twelve education—I had quit school early to join the navy—for me to graduate with my master's. I learned a few things in that time.

At first law school was hard. I tried to make sense of the material through my own cultural lens, and it didn't quite work. When I started looking at law the way I imagined a white male would look at it, it became much simpler. Law is deeply rooted in white Western thought.

If you come from a culture that does not automatically assume that property rights are natural, normal and necessary, you are going to struggle to understand decisions in bankruptcy law, real estate law, wills, trusts and international and criminal law.

If you come from a culture that is not dominated by a Christian monotheistic belief in one powerful, all-knowing, all-seeing, angry, punishing god, you will not automatically accept the principle of deterrence that is fundamental not only to criminal law but also to labour, human rights, tax and environmental law, as well as to all other areas where penalties and punishment are relied upon as though they are natural, normal and necessary.

If the people who write the law and the people who interpret the law and the people who teach the law are all from the same culture and share the same values, as they were when I went to law school, they do not have to fully explain their reasoning or ever question it. The decisions I studied in law school were written primarily by white male judges, and in writing their decisions they relied upon their own sense of propriety. Judges explain the rationale behind their decisions but often leave a great deal unsaid. The problem is that only people who share their particular cultural beliefs can fill in the blanks.

I struggled to make sense of law until I learned to fill in the blanks with what I knew from white Western industrial culture. Once I was able to do that, law became much easier to understand.

That's another thing I learned. You don't have to be smart to get through law school.

Law is not difficult. It's actually quite simple. Most of the professors I had were male. But male or female, when a human is given power over other humans, there is a tendency to abuse that power, and law professors are not exempt. I met more than a few who were bullies. Law professors have a lot of power in the classroom. They know the material and the students do not. Many of my professors had taught their course for years and even decades, and they had learned to anticipate students' questions and responses. They could stand at the front of the room and behave as though they had superior intelligence, when in fact all they had was the opportunity to learn the material before the students. Prior knowledge of the material put professors in a position where they could intimidate and ridicule students at will.

I had a professor who behaved like a peacock, strutting around and showing off in front of the class, inviting us to applaud his brilliance. In a personal exchange I told him, "Those who can, do. Those who can't, teach." Once I stood up to him and put him in his place he quit trying to impress me. I think my professors wanted the work they did to be important. They wanted people to think they were smart, so they complicated the courses they taught. It wasn't deliberate, I don't think. It's the story that held them: law is supposed to be hard. Courses such as bankruptcy and insolvency are taught as though they are complex, but the law in that area really isn't. There are a few rules and procedures to learn. There is some worthwhile history to know. But overall, the law around bankruptcy and insolvency has not changed much over the decades.

Criminal law doesn't require law professors to teach it. There are many people in jail who know as much about criminal law and procedure as the junior lawyers assigned to represent them. I have often seen people with personal experience in criminal law giving advice to accused persons in their communities, and they are certainly relied upon in correctional centres.

But law school is not about teaching law.

Law school is about making sure undesirable people do not enter the legal profession.

Law school is made unreasonably difficult—not because law is complex: it isn't. It's about maintaining the reputation that law is complex and that only a select few are capable of succeeding in the profession. Most courses in law end with three-hour exams worth 100 percent of the final grade. The practice of assigning 100 percent finals in law school is a deliberate stress magnifier. Students enter the examination room knowing that their performance during the next three hours will be the single determinant of success. It is not uncommon for people who have been out of law school for twenty or thirty years to wake up shaky and sweaty from nightmares about entering a law school examination in a panic because they hadn't studied.

I was thirty-five years old when I entered law school. I was confident. I was experienced. I was colonized sufficiently by my work in industry to be able to imagine going to law school. I had been on the negotiations team for my local union and gone up against the company to renegotiate our collective agreement. We had to call for a strike vote of our members before we concluded negotiations. And I knew how to work. I was accustomed to twelve-hour shifts in the mines. In law school I quickly learned that putting in twelve hours a day resulted in reasonable grades. If I put in more hours, my grades improved. I was also in the habit of showing up on time every day. I had spent several years working at a site where I knew the company wanted to fire me because of my activism and would fire me if I gave them the slightest reason. I had spent several years knowing that I would be fired if I came to work even a few minutes late. And so I was also familiar with stress. Yet even with the relative advantages my age and experience afforded me, I have a distinct memory of walking to law school one April morning and suffering wild mood swings—one moment I would be jubilant, filled with excitement and vigour, and the very next moment I'd be overcome with fear and anxiety. Excited one moment, afraid the next, back and forth, again and again. Stress is a killer.

The only thing law school taught me was how to write three-hour exams. I endured three years of intense study to learn a single skill that I would never use again. At no time during my twenty years of legal practice did I ever encounter a situation where the skill of writing examinations was an advantage.

Law school is not the bridge into the profession. It's the gate. It is there to keep people out. It's there to make sure poor people, women, Indigenous Peoples, single parents and other marginalized people do not make it through. It is designed by and for wealthy single white males.

The University of Saskatchewan offers a special class for Indigenous law students. It provides academic support. Students are taught essay writing and case briefing and are given tips on writing exams. I attended the class a few times but found that it was just additional work piled on an already unmanageable workload. It was more of a disadvantage than an advantage.

The Indigenous students that I knew in law school did not need academic support. We needed *life* support. We needed things like reliable daycare, affordable transportation and health services.

I remember one young Indigenous woman in first-year law school. We studied together and she was brilliant. Grace did not have problems understanding Western legal thinking. She was the one who told me to think like a white man and showed me that law was not difficult to understand. But she missed a lot of classes. The First Nation that she came from wanted to send as many people to university as possible, but they only had a small budget, so they gave each student half the amount needed in order to send twice as many students to university. Grace would have been far better off financially if she had quit school and gone on welfare. She had two young children. Daycare was not a problem because her mother moved in with her. But her mother was also taking care of a disabled son who required almost constant attention.

Grace's problem was that she didn't have enough money to feed herself, her children, her mother *and* her brother. She attended law school full-time to qualify for the funding from her First Nation. She had an outside job where she worked an additional forty hours a week. She was a mother to her children and assisted her mother in looking after her disabled brother. She lived in an apartment that was too small for five people and she could not come and take advantage of the quiet of the library to study because she was needed at home.

My friend did not need academic support. She didn't drop out because law was too complex for her to grasp. She didn't make it through law school because her life circumstances made it impossible for her to succeed.

In 2019, I spoke to Indigenous law students and a law professor friend at the University of Saskatchewan. They all assured me that other than mere tinkering, nothing substantial has changed at the law school I attended almost three decades ago. Law schools, in their arrogance, in their perpetuation of the myth that law is a complex body of thought, continue to assign exaggerated workloads, continue their abuse of students by elevating stress levels unnecessarily and continue to insultingly assign extra work to Indigenous and disadvantaged students and insinuate that the problem is that the students are not smart enough and require remedial assistance.

The practice of law does not require such an onerous regime of study that students are injured by stress. Law is not that complicated. Law schools simply maintain the fiction to maintain their prestige and to act as the gate to the profession.

2

*My experience suggests I didn't change the system;
it changed me.*

I CONFRONTED THE worst part of law school after
I graduated. Before admission into the law society and
the ceremony of being "called to the bar," prospective
lawyers must complete a year of articles under the
supervision of an approved senior lawyer. What made
my year of articles horrible wasn't the work. I articled
under Gerald Morin, an experienced Indigenous
lawyer with a thriving practice in Prince Albert. A fluent
Cree speaker, Gerry went on to serve as a provincial
court judge in Saskatchewan's Cree court. His style of
teaching was to throw me into the fire. The first week
I worked for him, he gave me an Employment Insurance
file. The client had been refused his claim. Gerry told

me that I would make the representations and that he would be behind me. The hearing was scheduled for a Friday. On the Wednesday I showed Gerry the arguments I had prepared. He approved, but apologized that he would not be able to accompany me on my first court appearance after all. I would have to do it on my own.

I showed up for the hearing a half-hour early because I wanted to see what the room looked like, to get my bearings. When I entered, another hearing, for a nurse's claim, was already in progress. The adjudicator, a gruff older man, interrupted the nurse's lawyer: "That's what I don't like about lawyers. You take too much time."

He then addressed the room: "Does anyone else here have a lawyer?"

I stood up and introduced myself as an articling student representing our client. The adjudicator then told me that I would be the last on the list for the day. He told the lawyer in the middle of his presentation to pack it all up and that he too could go to the end of the list. "These people have travelled a long way to be here today and I am not going to make them wait while lawyers waste time."

The adjudicator then proceeded to hear from the unrepresented people. He listened politely and frequently assured them he would see what he could do. When all the unrepresented were taken care of, he allowed the nurse's lawyer to continue his representation, but was brutal in his questioning.

Then it was my turn.

I thought I could win some favour by opening with an apology for any errors I might make and explaining that I was an articling student and that this was my first hearing. It didn't do me any good. The adjudicator challenged everything I said, demanding references for every fact I introduced. I had spent sufficient time in preparation to remember the page numbers in a very thick file, and was glad of it.

At one point I referred him to a particular paragraph central to my argument. I not only told him the page number, I also indicated that it was the third paragraph on the page and I began to read the first sentence to help him find it. Because the paragraph was so important, I decided to read the entire thing. It wasn't long, perhaps five sentences. When I finished, all he said was, "Now that was a complete waste of time, wasn't it."

I had never met anyone who behaved like that adjudicator. I had decades of experience in the navy and in heavy industry. I had dealt with the arrogance of military officers, foremen and mine captains, men who abused their authority, but none had been as belittling as that adjudicator. In the years to come, it would not be uncommon to meet judges who were simply mean, who bullied everyone who stood before them and who believed completely in their own superiority.

That first case wasn't complex. The facts were established, the arguments were straightforward. My client had been brutalized by his employer. The stress of his employment had been so extreme that he temporarily lost his vision. He needed effective representation. I could not allow myself to be distracted. It took effort not to be intimidated, but I stayed calm. The adjudicator ultimately decided in my client's favour, but for reasons other than those I presented.

Despite that first hearing, I probably had the most instructive and rewarding articling experience of anyone in my year, many of whom ended up carrying the briefcases of senior lawyers and were rarely afforded direct courtroom experience. I had ample opportunity to appear in court on a wide variety of matters: family law applications, criminal trials, real estate files, administrative law, Aboriginal and treaty law, and wills and estates. I assisted Gerry in a challenge to a municipal election, in which we represented an Indigenous man who had been elected a city councillor but whose opponent couldn't accept being beaten and assumed our client must have cheated. Gerry handily won this trial. The plaintiff showed himself to be merely vindictive and could offer no evidence of our client's misbehaviour.

Gerry even assigned me a murder file. It was an ugly file. The victim was a fourteen-year-old girl who had been raped, murdered and stuffed into a below-ground-level window well. The police were aided in their investigation by a young man who claimed he had found the body. Two Indigenous men were questioned and they both admitted to raping and murdering the young girl. They were charged and held in custody.

A DNA analysis—a relatively new procedure at the time—was conducted. When the results came back from the lab, they exonerated the two men who had confessed and indicated that the rapist was the young man who had been so helpful.

It bothered me that two men had confessed to a rape and murder they'd had nothing to do with. They had not been tortured by the police. The aggressive interviewing method of the police met the accepted standard. Their confessions would likely have been admissible at a trial. All their constitutional rights had been protected. Nothing could explain their confessions.

It was an invaluable lesson. I should have paid closer attention. Instead I treated that file as an anomaly. I went through my career as a lawyer, both as a defence counsel and a prosecutor, without ever satisfactorily answering the question: Why would someone admit to something they had not done? I encountered people who would claim that the convictions on their criminal records were inaccurate. That yes, they had been convicted and gone to prison, but they had not committed the offence. They had taken the rap for someone else, or they had pleaded guilty when they shouldn't have.

To prosecutors and judges, criminal records are sacrosanct. We fear calling into question previous convictions because the courts are already bogged down with today's accused, today's docket and today's trial schedule; adding the huge burden of reviewing historical errors would make things completely unmanageable.

Many times as a prosecutor I had people say to me, "Okay, I will just plead guilty then." Sometimes when I was really busy and not paying close attention, I might accept their plea. I admit, I probably did accept guilty pleas from people who were innocent. I prefer to think that I didn't, that when I recognized someone was taking responsibility for an offence they had not committed, I refused to accept their plea. But perhaps even then I unwittingly coerced them into pleading guilty. The usual interaction would go something like this:

Me: "Here is what the police said you did."

Accused: "Okay, I will just plead guilty then."

Me: "I can't accept that. If you are not taking responsibility, we'll have to go to a trial."

Pause.

Accused: "Okay then, yes, it was me. I did it."

And in front of the judge, he would say the magic words that I might have put in his mouth.

But back in that articling year, it was not just the judges who made things so difficult, not just the workload, not even the realization that the system is fallible. There was also my hatred of being poor.

I had left home at fifteen mostly because I hated being poor. When my father died and the government forced my mother off her trapline by threatening to take away her children, we moved to La Ronge to live on welfare. At the age of ten I discovered what poverty meant. We went from being wealthy, having everything we needed, including our independence, to being poor and waiting for a cheque to arrive every month. Five years later, I moved out and got a job. At seventeen, I joined the navy. When I came back I worked in mining and logging, which in the 1970s and '80s paid quite well. I became accustomed to earning a decent salary and paying my own way.

To pay for my first year of university, I used my savings and on weekends I worked in a plant that made fence posts. Later, I took out student loans and relied upon scholarships to get through law school and attend Harvard. Harvard is an expensive place to study. My Saskatchewan student loans, when converted into U.S. dollars, barely covered my rent. I delivered newspapers to earn enough money to eat. I also began a new family. My daughter Alita was born while we were in Cambridge. It was a struggle, yet we survived.

But by the time I was in my articling year, I was tired of being poor. The banks were after me to begin repaying my student loans, and I had a new family to support and child support to pay to my previous family. When my articles were done, I turned down Gerry's offer to practise in his office for the simple reason that I needed to earn more money than he could offer. I went back to mining for a bit.

Even though I hated being poor while I articled, that wasn't the most horrible part either. For me, the most horrible part was the realization that I had wasted five years of my life getting an education that was almost useless. Five years of being poor during which I could only provide minimally for my family, five years of not having the time to spend with my children, five years of hard work and stress levels that damaged my health, and in the end, none of it had prepared me for the practice of law.

To say that I was bitter would be an understatement. I was angry. I wanted to punch someone, to kick something, to curse and swear and scream and rip my hair out. In law school we studied court of appeal and Supreme Court decisions and explored abstract concepts in critical legal thinking and none of it taught me a damn thing about the practice of law. I didn't know how to interview a client. I didn't know how to negotiate a settlement with opposing counsel. I didn't know how to present myself in court. I didn't know anything about the business of running a law office. Most of the stuff that lawyers need to know to practise law is not taught in law school. Law school never prepared me for the woman crying in my office. It didn't teach me what to say when her husband phoned me at home in the middle of the night to ask me if she was paying me with blow jobs because she certainly didn't have any money.

The important stuff—like how to do research, how to find a decision, how precedent works, and enough legal theory to understand that law is just something we made up and continue to make up as we go along—could be taught to anyone in less than a year. It could be taught in a trade school, and it probably should be taught in a trade school along with mechanics and plumbing.

Canada went through a recession in the early 1980s. One winter when work was scarce, I went to a trade school and studied heavy equipment mechanics. The teaching was mostly hands-on, tearing engines and transmissions apart to see what was inside, with some classroom time to study the fundamentals. Looking back, comparing law school to trade school, I am forced to conclude that trade school actually taught me more, and what it taught me had substance. I continue to use the skills I acquired in trade school; they come in handy when I have a problem with my vehicle. Very little of what I was forced to study in law school has any applicability in the real world.

I had thought that going to Harvard would give me some advantage in the practice of law. It didn't. Attending one of the most renowned universities in the world didn't help me in the courtroom. In fact, it might have been a disadvantage. Judges, prosecutors and opposing counsel knew I had been to Harvard and expected me to make brilliant arguments because of it. Most often, though, all I could muster were the same mundane arguments that everyone else presented. An extra year of study and a prestigious degree only gave me more insight into abstract concepts that have little to no applicability in court. On those rare occasions when I could incorporate some of the concepts I learned in law school into a legal argument, I was usually met with judges who were either incapable of grasping the concepts, or could not see their applicability to the case in front of them. I quickly learned not to make those arguments.

One of the solutions proposed to improve the condition of Indigenous people within the justice system is to increase the number of Indigenous lawyers and judges. But my experience suggests I didn't change the system; it changed me. To become lawyers, most of us will have experienced seven or more years of post-secondary indoctrination. To be successful in university, we will have bought into a host of principles. We will have learned and accepted concepts that are peculiar to the dominant culture. Our intellect will be altered. We will have learned to think like a settler. Admission to a university requires a high school diploma, so we can add on another twelve years of conditioning. By the time we enter the courtroom, most of us will have spent almost twenty years outside of our culture and much of that time will have been spent outside our communities. We will be changed.

3

I was perpetuating both the system and the suffering.

BY THE TIME we receive our call to the bar, when we go to the office of the law society and swear the oath and sign the book, very little of our Indigenous identity remains. We tend to perceive ourselves as successful. We are proud of our achievements, our degrees, our acceptance into an elite society. And we should be. We should be proud. After all those years of hard study and sacrifice and dedication, we beat the odds. We stand up straight. We did it. We are finally someone.

Then we come back into our communities and are reminded of where we came from. We are ashamed of the poverty and the violence and the hopelessness.

We ask ourselves, Why can't they do like we did? Why can't they dig themselves out of this mess? There must be something wrong with them. They must be lazy.

These were quiet voices at the back of my mind when I went home in 2002. I tried to ignore them as I went about my business. I intended to live with my wife, Joan, in my cabin on my trapline, taking on research projects for income. As a researcher with government contracts I would not need to belong to the law society and so wouldn't need to pay their annual fees. I went to La Ronge to have a lawyer swear a document declaring my withdrawal from the law society. Bill Brown was the only private-practice lawyer in town. He convinced me that the town needed another private-practice lawyer and promised that if I opened an office he would help. He gave me a new fax machine that he didn't like. He preferred his old one that used shiny paper. He said that once I opened an office, for the first six months I wouldn't have enough to do, for the next six months I would have enough work, and for the six months after that I would wish I was back in the first six months again.

His prediction was dead-on accurate. But it wasn't the potential success of the business alone that convinced me. Bill emphasized that the area's residents deserved to have access to legal representation and he was not able to provide all that was needed. Bill was at the end of his career. He had been forced to resign from legal aid upon turning seventy, something he was still bitter about in his eighties.

The greater La Ronge area encompasses the Lac La Ronge Indian Band, the town of La Ronge, the village of Air Ronge and the Northern Municipal Administration that is responsible for cottage areas and the golf course. The total combined population is close to eight thousand, and more than half that number are members of the Lac La Ronge Indian Band. La Ronge is on the southern edge of the Precambrian Shield, on the shore of Lac la Ronge, or Mistahi-Sâkahikanihk (Big Lake). The town is the administrative centre for northern Saskatchewan, with a hospital, colleges, hotels, restaurants, a courthouse and a large provincial government presence, including the district prosecution and legal aid offices. Forty years ago it was a tourist destination, but today it is only a stopping-off point for the more remote locations preferred for fishing camps.

La Ronge is the last place people heading farther north can legally buy alcohol, and the town boasts a government liquor store and several bars, lounges and off-sale outlets. People living beyond La Ronge purchase their alcohol here and transport it back to their home communities for their own consumption or to resell. A twenty-six-ounce bottle of whiskey can sell for up to $150 in a Far North community.

The median annual income for northern Saskatchewan was $16,860 in 2016, compared with $28,792 for the whole of Saskatchewan. Some northern communities have a median annual income as low as $6,107. Twenty-two percent of northern income is by way of government transfer; in some communities this figure creeps as high as 47 percent. The biggest non-government employer used to be the mining sector, but with low uranium prices most of the mines have now shut down. The north as a whole has a long-term unemployment rate of about 10 percent, whereas province-wide the rate is 3 percent. In some communities more than three-quarters of the houses require major repairs, and over-crowding is widespread. The population of northern Saskatchewan is roughly thirty-eight thousand, of whom 85 percent are Indigenous, and 99 percent of the people who show up in court as accused persons are Indigenous.

It felt good when Joan and I opened a law office in the town of La Ronge in 2004. I had a purpose; I was providing a service. I took on a few family law files and some real estate files, but the vast majority of the files I took were criminal. At first I felt I was doing something good: I was keeping my clients out of jail. For most of them, any sentence that was not a jail sentence was a victory. And if a jail sentence was inevitable, then I fought hard for the shortest possible term of incarceration.

I was fortunate to practise law in La Ronge, where the prosecutors and defence lawyers got along with each other. There are other communities where the animosity is extreme. I was also in a community where I was well known. Most of my clients had an income and so did not qualify for legal aid, but they could not afford to pay for the big law firms in the southern cities. They could, however, afford me.

Criminal law is mostly about negotiations. Major crimes—first-degree murder, aggravated sexual assault—tend to go to trial more frequently than less serious matters, but the sentences for even these are often negotiated. If it were not for the plea bargain process, the entire administration of criminal law would grind to a halt as the courts became overwhelmed. Only a few matters are scheduled for trial, and of those many are settled either before the trial begins, often on the way into the courtroom on the first day of the trial, or partway through the trial, when either the prosecutor or the defence counsel have a clearer view of the evidence. Trials are risky for both sides. No matter how well you prepare, you never know what a witness is going to say until they have said it on the stand. Negotiations and witness preparation are not taught in law school. These are skills lawyers learn on the job and with experience can be mastered by just about anyone.

As defence counsel, all I needed to do at trial was raise a reasonable doubt. I had one client who was accused of fondling his teenage daughter. At trial, under my cross-examination, the daughter admitted that she had been pressured by her mother and by Child and Family Services to go to the police and give a statement and that she had been pressured to attend court that day to testify. That pressure was enough for the judge to doubt the veracity of her testimony, and my client was acquitted. The acquittal didn't mean my client hadn't done what he was accused of. All the verdict meant was that the case against him had not been proven successfully. As defence counsel, I considered the verdict a success. But to the community, and to the family and the daughter, it might not have been.

Early in my private practice I was hired by a young man in a northern community. He had been charged with assault and uttering threats. It was alleged that he had gone to his former partner's residence, pushed and slapped her, smashed a chair and threatened to come back and do more damage. My client admitted he'd gone to his ex's residence to pick up their daughter. When his ex refused to allow him to take the ten-year-old girl, there were a few heated words and then he left. He told me he did not strike his ex-partner and he did not break a chair. The police report contained a recorded statement by the complainant and photographs of a smashed chair.

My client insisted I talk to the little girl. She had been there. She had witnessed it all. It was a hard situation to put her in. It was bad enough that her family was torn apart and her parents were not getting along, but here she was, being asked to choose between the two most important people in her young life. She was very shy, very quiet, and spoke with her head down. She told me that her mother had been upset when her father had come to collect her because she believed he had entered into a new relationship. Both parents had sworn at each other, and then her father had left. After he was gone, her mother smashed a chair and phoned the RCMP. The little girl did not want to go to court, did not want to speak in public. It was difficult enough that she had told me. I could only imagine what it would feel like for her to be forced to testify—to stand before a roomful of people, not only those from her community who would gossip but also the strangers who would administer punishment—and publicly betray her mother.

At first the prosecutor insisted he would listen to the couple's daughter only if she was on the witness stand. I understood his position. All prosecutors in Saskatchewan are mandated to vigorously prosecute all domestic violence charges. It took a lot of persuading to get him to talk to the girl outside the courtroom, and he agreed to do so only if my client, whom he believed was manipulating his daughter, was not in the interview room. Going into the meeting, the prosecutor told me he was not inclined to believe the girl. How frightened she must have been alone in a room with a stranger whose body language probably conveyed his doubt. However, when the prosecutor came out of the room, he agreed to withdraw the charge.

Every sentence administered in provincial court results in collateral damage in the community. Every trial traumatizes the victims who are forced to testify (or are charged with an offence if they refuse). That time a little girl did not have to testify; she was not put on public display and humiliated. She was bruised by her experience, but she wasn't seriously injured. It could have been different. She might have carried the guilt of her betrayal for many years. It might have destroyed her relationship with her mother, and she might have excluded herself from the few positive things in her community.

Except in the rarest of circumstances, criminal legal procedure does not take into account the community. I was hired by a man who, along with his adult sons, was accused of drunkenly breaking into his neighbours' house and attacking them while they slept. There was a mountain of circumstantial evidence and the coherent and consistent statements that several witnesses gave to the police. The prosecutor knew he had a strong case and he was not looking to settle. If my client were convicted of a home invasion, there was little chance that I could keep him out of prison.

On the day of the trial, I spoke to the main accuser, a young man I knew to be fair-minded and not prone to seeking revenge. He did not want my client to go to prison either. He knew my client worked in the mines and that if he went to prison, he would lose his job and his family would suffer. But at the same time he wanted my client to both sober up and take responsibility. Despite the initial position of the prosecutor, his main witness—who was also the victim—and I were able to persuade him to agree to a sentencing circle. There, my client pleaded guilty and the victims told him how his actions had affected them. They wanted him to pay for the damages, stay sober, quit acting tough and focus on looking after his family. The judge agreed with the rec-ommendations of the circle, and my client was given a two-year conditional sentence that required him to not drink or possess alcohol. To my knowledge he has never been in conflict with the law again.

But those types of community wins were rare. I had a client who hired me to defend him on a spousal assault charge. He paid my fee and expenses, and I flew into a remote community and beat the charge. He hit her again, and again he hired me, and again I beat the charge for him. Then he hit her a third time and sent me my fee. And it occurred to me then, the son of a bitch thinks he can hit his wife any time he wants and Harold Johnson will come and rescue him. This time when I got there, I took him out behind the community hall where we were holding court and told him, "If you hit her again, buddy, I am going to kick the shit out of you. Now get in there and plead guilty and I'll do what I can to keep your sorry ass out of jail."

It was cases like this that made me leave my practice. Although I kept a few people out of jail, or helped them get reduced sentences, I view my time as defence counsel as a failure. I did not help my community. The crime rate did not go down. Life did not improve in the community, and after a while I began to feel like a parasite feeding off the suffering. All I was doing was maintaining the status quo. I was perpetuating both the system and the suffering.

4

As a prosecutor, there were no community-based sanctions available to me.

I TOLD MYSELF I must be on the wrong side. And so I went to work as a prosecutor, and there I faced a dilemma.

From the regional prosecutions office in La Ronge, four prosecutors covered the fly-in circuit of ten communities in the northeastern and far northern parts of the province. I was the only Indigenous prosecutor in the region—when I started and when I retired. The vast majority of people I prosecuted were Indigenous, and in many cases I pushed for incarceration. I told myself that because the victims were also Indigenous, I wasn't so much prosecuting fellow Indigenous people as I was defending Indigenous victims. I told myself that I was protecting the community. The community needed a break from the offender's bad behaviour. I told myself that our traditional form of dealing with bad behaviour was banishment and that jail was simply a modern form of banishment. I told myself that I wasn't relying upon principles of deterrence or punishment, because I knew neither was effective, but rather I was recommending jail to separate the offender from the victims and thus maintaining peace in the community. It was a good story. It helped me go to work every day.

But like everyone else in the administration of justice, I did not allow myself to consider what would happen when the offender was released from custody and returned to the community. The truth, though, builds up. Over time it becomes harder and harder to maintain the story.

I didn't learn about trauma and its impact until after I quit prosecuting, and yet now I understand that so much of what I confronted as a lawyer, no matter which side I was on, was the product of trauma. Trauma is real. Given the historical trauma of residential school, coupled with the extreme violence that permeates some of our communities, trauma is a fact of life for many Indigenous people. There had been a residential school in La Ronge until it mysteriously burned down in 1947. Then it was moved south to Prince Albert, where it operated until 1997. I met the survivors in court, and I met their children and their grandchildren.

Trauma occurs when a person experiences an event that triggers the fight, flight or freeze response, only the response doesn't go away once the event is over. More and more people appearing before the courts are themselves the victims of trauma. The symptoms of post-traumatic stress disorder, or PTSD, are hyper-vigilance, anxiety, depression, worry and heightened fight, flight or freeze reactions. People with PTSD who are triggered can react with extreme violence. Their actions lack intention. Not only do they not plan to react violently; they do not have time to think about their actions beforehand. According to world-renowned trauma expert Bessel van der Kolk, "To people who are reliving a trauma, nothing makes sense; they are trapped in a life-or-death situation, a state of paralyzing fear or blind rage. Mind and body are constantly aroused, as if they are in imminent danger. They startle in response to the slightest noises and are frustrated by small irritations. Their sleep is chronically disturbed, and food often loses its sensual pleasures. This in turn can trigger desperate attempts to shut those feelings

down by freezing and dissociation."[1] We have traumatized people in our communities who are committing
atrocities and traumatizing themselves even more. We
then bring these people into the justice system and
force them through a preliminary hearing and a trial,
adding to their trauma. Then we send them to jail,
where we can be sure they will be severely traumatized. Eventually we release them back into their communities and ask them if they learned their lesson.

As a prosecutor, there were no community-based
sanctions available to me, and so I would ask the presiding judge to incarcerate these offenders. I reasoned,
"These people are so unhealthy, they are a danger to
themselves or to others." This was not a solution that
restored good health. It was a shortcut.

As a Crown prosecutor I prosecuted around fifteen
hundred files a year. Roughly a thousand of those documented trauma—not just the trauma the offender
was suffering but also the woman who was beaten and
the five children who watched. Multiply my one thousand files by eleven prosecutors in this territory and
each year we had eleven thousand files each docu-
menting multiple traumas. And there were only thirty-
eight thousand people in this territory. It doesn't take
very many years before this population is traumatized
multiple times.

It is not just the offenders, the victims and the witnesses to crimes who are traumatized. Police officers frequently experience PTSD as a result of their work. Two stories come to mind that were told to me by officers. The first was a male officer assigned to a remote northern community. He and his partner were called to a house where a man was drunk and causing trouble. The officers attempted to arrest him, and he resisted. While they were wrestling with the man on the living room floor trying to put him in handcuffs, the officer who told me the story looked up. There were three little boys sitting on the couch watching television, leaning over to see around the scuffle and continuing to watch their cartoons. That image bothered this officer so much that he left the force.

The second story was told to me by a female officer who had been called to a house where something horrible had obviously happened. The walls and the floor were covered in blood. The furniture was smashed and there were broken things everywhere. What traumatized this officer, too, were the children in the house. This time they were six or seven years old and came up to her to ask if she had any of the stickers that the police routinely hand out to children as part of their community-building practice. Like the first officer, she wondered whether the violence in their lives was

so routine that the children didn't even notice it anymore. She asked to be transferred out of the north.

More than three hundred police officers are
assigned to this territory—that's one officer for every
126 people. Many of these officers have been traumatized by the violence they have witnessed and perpe-
trated. When we have a traumatized and inflated
police force interacting with a traumatized population,
we should not expect good results. The Ontario city of
Timmins has a larger population but only about eighty
officers, or one for every five hundred or so people.
Rimouski in Quebec and Grande Prairie in Alberta
also have larger populations. Imagine if any of these
small cities had police forces of more than three hundred officers. With that many officers patrolling and
investigating, there would be far more arrests and
charges laid.

A staff sergeant in command of a northern community ordered his officers to lay every possible charge for
every event. It was his hope that, if the number of
charges laid in that community went up, an additional
officer would be assigned there. That staff sergeant was
transferred when his plan became known. But it's not
just police who know that more charges mean more
police. Community leaders often rely upon charge
rates, as well as increasing levels of violence in their

communities, to demand more officers. Of course the more officers in a community, the more charges will be laid, and the more charges that are laid spirals into meaning more officers are assigned. Yet it seems to me that asking for more police to fix a broken community is like asking for more buckets to fix a leaking roof.

A few people from this region have joined the RCMP, but they are never assigned to their home community. Most RCMP officers here are non-Indigenous, and they do not understand the culture of or the trauma suffered by the people they are meant to serve. For the most part they do not understand their own trauma, either.

We have a distinct shortage of counsellors, and those that are here tell me they are overwhelmed. Corey O'Soup, Saskatchewan's advocate for children and youth, has said that it can take up to two years for a child in the province to see a counsellor. We would be much better off if instead of three hundred police officers we had three hundred trauma counsellors.

5

In northern Saskatchewan, alcohol is the elephant in the room.

IN THE ABSENCE of proper treatment, many people self-medicate with alcohol. If you are a business person in one of our larger cities, you might have a stress level of two or three. You go out on a Friday and have a few drinks and your stress level goes down to zero. If you experience symptoms of PTSD—anxiety, depression and an overwhelming sense of loss—your stress level is seven, eight or nine. You go out and have a few drinks and your stress level goes down to two or three and that feels good. You want to be there all the time. That's what you think normal feels like.

Alcohol is very good at ameliorating the symptoms of PTSD. The problem is the side effects. A person quickly develops a tolerance and requires more and more alcohol to achieve the same results, and of course alcohol is intoxicating and impairs motor skills and judgment. In my experience, 95 percent of the people I prosecuted were intoxicated when they committed the offence that landed them in court.

Not too long ago I was at the picnic table behind the government building in La Ronge where I had worked as a prosecutor. I was having a visit with Rick Bell. Rick has over thirty years' experience as defence counsel, practising primarily criminal law. Near the end of our conversation, Rick said, "You know, I have only ever represented one man charged with murder who was sober at the time." I thought about that for a moment and agreed—I too had only ever prosecuted one man who was sober when he committed a murder. "But when it comes to sex assault," Rick said, "never." That also was my experience. I had never prosecuted a sexual assault charge that did not involve alcohol. And in a discussion with Erin Layton, then a legal aid lawyer working out of La Ronge, about domestic violence, between us we could recall only one man in all of northern Saskatchewan who was known to regularly beat his partner when he was sober. The Ontario Domestic Assault Risk Assessment is a widely used tool to measure risk when the victim is a domestic partner. Data from 2015 to 2018 shows that 94.74 percent of all domestic violence in the La Ronge region involved alcohol.

In northern Saskatchewan, alcohol is the elephant in the room. It is the truth we all know and agree not to talk about. Despite alcohol's implication in the majority of offending, it receives very little attention from those of us involved in the administration of justice. Judges issue orders that require offenders to refrain from drinking and possessing alcohol. It is not uncommon for a probation order or a conditional sentence order to contain a clause requiring the offender to attend alcohol counselling and treatment. But that is the extent of the attention paid to an overwhelming problem. The administrators of law—judges, prosecutors, defence counsel and attorneys general—have not directly addressed alcohol, even though it is involved in most of the files, even though it is in our courts and in our faces every day.

Maybe we don't discuss alcohol because of section 33.1 of the Criminal Code. This section stipulates that self-induced intoxication is not a defence to a charge of assault or interference with the bodily integrity of a person.[2] And according to the Supreme Court, "there is no threshold of intoxication beyond which s. 33.1 . . . does not apply to an accused."[3] No matter how drunk a person becomes, it can never be a defence that they did not have the intention to commit an assault or especially a sexual assault.

The vast majority of cases involving violence dealt with by the courts are covered by section 33.1. As defence counsel and later as a prosecutor, I mostly dealt with assaults—assaults with a weapon, assaults causing bodily harm, aggravated assaults, and sexual assaults, as well as breaches of court orders arising from these charges. As defence counsel, I only tried to raise the defence of intoxication once (and failed), and I never encountered it as a prosecutor. My client had consumed so much alcohol that he blacked out. I hired an expert to explain to the court that if my client was so intoxicated that his brain no longer func-tioned enough to store memories, then he was also so intoxicated that he could not form the required inten-tion to be guilty of a crime. The judge didn't accept the expert's evidence and my client was convicted.

Maybe the reason those of us in the administration of justice rarely discuss alcohol is because the defence is rarely raised. Maybe . . .

Or maybe the reason we don't talk about alcohol is because in our world the use of alcohol has become so natural, normal and maybe even necessary that to dis-cuss it would be like discussing the floor or the walls. It's the background noise.

Maybe the reason we never talk about alcohol is because alcohol is so widely used. In 2013, in Canada, 80.6 percent of men and 71.2 percent of women used alcohol at risky levels, according to the 2015 *Chief Public Health Officer's Report on the State of Public Health in Canada*. Risky drinking is defined in that report as more than three drinks a day for men or more than fifteen drinks in a week, and more than two drinks a day for women or more than ten drinks a week. If close to three-quarters of Canadians are regularly using alcohol at risky levels, then close to three-quarters of the judges, prosecutors, defence counsel and others involved in the administration of justice must also be using alcohol at those levels. It is very hard to be critical of something you are using or possibly abusing.

As a prosecutor, I used to fly in to remote communities where we held court with the judge, defence counsel, the court clerk and sometimes a probation officer. We would spend an entire day dealing with people who had gotten drunk and done something wrong, some to devastating effect. We flew in and cleaned up after the party, and there was a lot of cleaning up to do—broken teeth, smashed windows, sexual assaults, physical assaults, impaired driving, impaired driving causing bodily harm or death. Most of the break and enters we dealt with were committed by people who broke in to steal alcohol.

Then at the end of the day we would climb back on board the chartered aircraft to fly home. It is part of the contract the airline has with the province's department of justice that drinks are supplied for these flights. As each person entered the aircraft, they'd usually stop at the cooler at the back of the plane and select a beverage, mostly beer or wine, but there was always a bottle of expensive single malt Scotch on offer as well. They drank on the flight back, and upon arriving at the home airport, got into their vehicles and drove home.

They didn't seem to make any connection between the alcohol on the plane and the alcohol in the communities they had just left. They didn't connect the devastation they witnessed all day with the bottle or glass in their hand. No matter how often we made that flight and regardless of the horrors we witnessed, the connection was never made.

Perhaps this lack of association was based upon racist assumptions—only Indians drink to wild excess. Or perhaps a more benign assumption, that only people with drinking problems drink like that. Yet in those remote courts, of the 95 percent of accused who were intoxicated when they committed their offence, I would estimate that only 15 to 20 percent of them were what I refer to as obsessive-compulsive drinkers—people who either could not or would not stop drinking. My estimate is based purely upon observation, but it is supported by evidence. Seventy percent of the alcohol consumed in Canada is consumed by 20 percent of the population. Or, to break that down a little more, 10 percent of the population consumes 40 percent of the alcohol.[4]

These extreme drinkers did end up in court occasionally, but they were not generally the problem. They typically spent all of their time finding the resources to get a bottle, and once they had it, they found someplace safe to drink it. They usually came to court when someone beat them up and took their bottle or molested them when they were passed out.

Most of the people I saw in court were not in that category. They were not addicted or obsessive-compulsive drinkers. They just got drunk and did something stupid. You don't have to be addicted to alcohol to drink too much, get in your car and kill someone. You don't have to be addicted to alcohol to drink too much and get in a fight, or to make a really stupid mistake about whether the woman you want to seduce is consenting or not. The problem with alcohol-induced criminality is not addiction. It's intoxication.

When I was prosecuting, every day I heard the refrain, "When he's sober he's a good guy. It was just the alcohol." I heard this assertion most often from women who had had the shit kicked out of them. For the first few years, I told myself these women were just making excuses for their abusers, that their insistence on the goodness of these guys was part of the cycle of violence. But after hearing the same thing over and over and over again, these women coming to court, telling me it was just the alcohol, asking me to drop the charges or to find some way to keep the accused out of jail, I began to listen.

What I found was that these men were mostly good guys. Yes, there were some extreme cases, men who deserved to be sent away, but for the most part I was dealing with people who simply got drunk and did something stupid. A typical example is the guy who got drunk and created a disturbance. The police arrived and tried to arrest him, and he became belligerent, fighting, swearing, calling the police racists, and the police had a struggle getting him into the police vehicle, taking him to the detachment and placing him in a cell, where he screamed and yelled and kicked at the door until he passed out. The next morning, he was a completely different person. He was quiet, he was polite, he apologized for his behaviour and seemed genuinely ashamed of his actions. This is the guy I saw in court. Depending upon the officers involved, I was often told they wouldn't mind if I stayed or withdrew the charges. I did not need the police's agreement before I withdrew a charge, but it was much easier if I had it.

6

Redemption is important not just at sentencing,
it's fundamental to well-being.

THE ADMINISTRATION OF justice is supposed to
be impartial. We are not supposed to bring our own
emotions into our decisions. But we are human and we
have emotions. I've seen obviously angry judges make
decisions. I've seen emotional defence counsel pleading for their clients. I was not immune. I prosecuted
a case in which the five-year-old victim had serious
bite marks over most of his body. As I looked through
the photos, my anger rose. I was tempted to agree to the
accused's release from custody just so that I could get
my hands on him in the parking lot. I wanted to show
him what pain felt like. Instead I went for a walk and
calmed myself down. Then I went into the courthouse

and insisted upon a lengthy term of incarceration. It was all I could do.

Most of the people who appear in court would be better dealt with by some alternative to incarceration, by finding some way for them to earn redemption. (There will always be those who are a danger to themselves and to others, and for them, incarceration remains the best available solution.) If you are an Indigenous person, your defence counsel will likely invoke the Gladue principles at sentencing. The Supreme Court in 1999 decided the case of R. v. Gladue wherein it determined that a judge sentencing an Aboriginal offender must consider the unique circumstances of Aboriginal Peoples and consider all sanctions other than jail available in the community. The problem with R. v. Gladue is that there are very few alternatives to custody available in the community, so defence counsel will hammer away at the unique circumstances hoping to obtain a shorter jail sentence for their client.

Upon a guilty plea, the prosecutor will read into the record an agreed statement of facts: what the accused admits to doing. The prosecutor may recommend a sentence. Then defence counsel gets up and tells the court about their client. They go through the list: poverty, dislocated community, unemployment, addictions, colonialism, family breakdown, residential school, violence, sexual and physical abuse and foster homes. By the time defence counsel has finished, everyone believes that the offender is the victim and we all forget about the people who have been hurt by this person's actions.

The worst part is, we have now convinced the offender that he is a victim. It's not his fault. He acted the way he did because of colonialism, failed government policy, unemployment, residential school and poverty. And if it wasn't his fault, then he does not need to make amends. Since he is a victim, it's not up to him to fix things. (I use "he" for offender and "she" for victim because that was the most common situation I encountered, but of course women can be offenders as well and men can be victims.)

It's easy to convince people who come out of communities of hopelessness that they are not responsible, that they never had a chance to begin with. The hard part is convincing them that they should take responsibility for their actions, that they should work at redemption, that they are responsible for the state their community is in and that they should make redress to their victim or victims.

Those circumstances of colonialism, unemployment, residential school and poverty are real and are often the status quo in our communities, and even though the Supreme Court did not include trauma in its decision, we can add it to the list. These circumstances are to be dealt with at all levels of society—education, health, family services, industry, environment, local community administration and justice. But simply using them as a means of shifting blame fails to ameliorate them in any way. Those rare times in court when I saw offenders take responsibility for their actions and accept whatever penalty the judge imposed on them, I also knew that I was not likely to see that person in court again. Those people came in, said, "I did wrong," apologized, accepted the penalty and walked out of the courtroom with dignity. They left as whole human beings, not as victims, and they earned the respect of the court. Redemption is important not just at sentencing—how is this person going to make things right in his or her community?—it's fundamental to well-being.

I am familiar with a community that suffered widespread sexual abuse that went on for decades. I am whispered to that there was an Elder, now dead, who is estimated to have had more than a hundred victims. He was never reported. He was never charged. And he wasn't the only one. It was a thing. Young men openly preyed upon vulnerable women. In the 1980s family workers became aware of the situation and began to investigate. Community leaders shut them down. Nobody wanted to talk about what was happening. And so the cauldron continued to boil. Today the community must contend with a suicide epidemic, and a police officer there tells me it is the most violent community he has ever been assigned to. Until a few years ago alcohol was the go-to drug. But a forest fire forced the evacuation of the community, and three weeks later people returned from the south with crystal meth, and now that drug is rampant.

I once asked a knowledge keeper why it was that we had people who were obviously drinking themselves to death, who knew that alcohol was going to kill them and continued to drink regardless. He told me that they had done something they could not forgive themselves for. And we know that the more alcohol that is consumed by a population, the higher the incidence of violence, including sexual assault.

Justice cannot fix this. When a community becomes mired in sexual abuse, both historical and present-day, the symptoms are increased use of substances and community fragmentation as people stop trusting each other. Justice has nothing to offer such a community. Sending a victimizer to jail ignores that this person might also be the victim of sexual abuse. There is no safe way for a justice system dependent upon punishment to intervene in the cycle. All it can do is take a hurt person and hurt them more.

For both settlers and Indigenous Peoples, the vast majority of sexual assaults are never reported to the police. The victims are often ashamed, or blame themselves. They are also traumatized. Their brains could not form coherent memories while the assault occurred. Afterwards they are frightened and confused. Because of such trauma, victims of sexual assault make very poor witnesses.

Victims who do come forward are publicly embarrassed by being forced to testify, treated as victims instead of as individuals by the prosecution, and demeaned and ridiculed by defence counsel. And when the courts are done with them, they are tossed out to fend for themselves. If they are damaged by the process, they must find their own therapy. The courts have no further use for them.

Rarely does the court find a fitting solution. If the accused is found guilty, then the court will punish him. That doesn't help the woman who was brutalized. Sending him to jail doesn't fix the things he broke—not just lips and teeth and ribs but pride and dignity and self-worth as well. We tell ourselves that is not our job—our job is to do law, and law is not about mental health counselling or social work.

As an example, I will put myself in the position of the victim who doesn't want to go to court and testify. When I was about ten years old, I was sexually assaulted by an older man in my community. Shortly after that assault, I was sexually assaulted by a schoolteacher. I never told anyone. The only person I could talk to about it was myself, and I told my ten-year-old self that the only reason these men had done what they'd done was because I did not have a father. I was angry and bitter for a long time and beat up other kids for no reason other than they had fathers and I didn't.

I eventually found my way beyond my anger and bitterness, buried the episode and lived my life. Now, fifty years later, if I were to decide to pursue charges against those two men, I would first have to go to a police station and give a statement to a police officer. Because the offence is a sexual assault, the assigned officer must complete a Violent Crime Linkage Analysis System form, asking very detailed questions about the abuse. If I can accurately remember what happened five decades ago and convince the officer that I am telling the truth and not just making this up as a publicity stunt so that I can sell more books, the officer will forward the file to a prosecutor. I will then have to convince the prosecutor that I am telling the truth. Once I have convinced the prosecutor by telling my story again, I will be subpoenaed to give evidence at a preliminary inquiry. Here I will tell my story for a third time, and this time I will be cross-examined by defence counsel who know that if they beat me up sufficiently at this preliminary stage then I might not come back for the trial. If there is a trial, I will tell the story for a fourth time and will again be attacked by defence counsel, who will try to show the judge or jury either that I am making everything up or that my memory is faulty or a combination of both.

I won't expect that either of the accused will plead guilty. A sexual assault upon a child is viewed as such a horrendous crime that they are not likely to admit to it. And if they were to admit what they did to me, they would know that the shortest possible sentence for any sexual assault, as determined by the Saskatchewan Court of Appeal, is three years in prison.

Let's assume that I have successfully convinced the police officer, the prosecutor, the judge at the preliminary inquiry and the judge or jury at the trial. Even if I haven't triggered my trauma, if I haven't become angry and bitter again and reacted violently to people with fathers or sought relief in alcohol or opiates, I am still in a worse position than if I had done nothing.

The best that the courts can do if the two men are convicted of committing sexual assault is to sentence them to jail. Jail doesn't help me. Punishing those two men by sending them away doesn't assist me with the trauma of the original assault or the aggravated trauma of the court process. Yes, there are victim services, but they are designed to arrange transportation and accommodation so the victim can attend court. Victim services will not offer trauma therapy either before or after the court process.

Once I have finished testifying, the court will throw me back to fend for myself. It will have provided me with nothing and it will have made my situation worse.

I am a man and I am well educated, I am very familiar with how the courts work, and I would not want to go through the process.

7

*Going to a white man's court and testifying against
a community member feels like betrayal.*

WITNESSES EVEN TO the most tragic of events are
reluctant to testify. Often what I encountered among
potential witnesses was an unwillingness to cooperate
with a foreign system. Going to a white man's court
and testifying against a community member feels like
betrayal of one's people.

Court in northern communities takes place once
or twice a month. The court plane flies in, bringing a
judge, a prosecutor, a legal aid lawyer, a clerk and
sometimes a probation officer. We landed at the airport if there was an airport, or with skis or floats on
the lake if there wasn't. During breakup and freeze-
up, when planes cannot land on the lake, we flew in

like rock stars in a helicopter. The RCMP were there to meet us, and we loaded our briefcases in the back of the truck and piled in for the ride to the band office or community hall where we would hold court for the day.

We were a strange sight in our suits, ties and other southern apparel. We not only looked white; we dressed more white than white. I once asked Saskatchewan's chief judge why as an Indigenous person I was required to wear a suit and tie, the dress of an elite European, before I could appear in court. He didn't have an answer.

There is a government restriction on travel when the temperature falls below minus thirty degrees Celsius. If, on the morning before we left our larger southern centres, the temperature was minus thirty-one, either at our point of departure or our destination, court would be cancelled. It might seem like a safe, rational thing to do, but in northern communities of people familiar with living on the land, a temperature of minus thirty is a rather pleasant winter day. We only appeared more foreign with our fear of winter weather.

We were outsiders and for the most part we behaved as such. We would spend little time in the community other than in the building where court was held. We might go to a restaurant for lunch, if the community had a restaurant, and when we got there we would all sit together, often along with the RCMP officer who drove us. Very rarely did we attend a community event, not more than once a year. I recall one Treaty Day celebration at Hatchet Lake First Nation. A large tent had been set up and lunch was being served to the community. I was disappointed to learn that I was lining up for hamburgers and hotdogs. I happened to look through a gap and saw people behind the tent cooking fish over an open fire. I took my plate and arrived just as someone was taking a whitefish off the fire. I was invited to share it with him. I noted that when the cook took his portion, he left the head. I asked him if it was okay if I took it. My desire to eat a fish head won the approval of the people there. Someone brought out a large trout head that had earlier been left aside, split it and put it on the fire. Trout heads are among the best-tasting heads of any fish in this territory. I was asked to stay and help eat it when it was done. I was a bit late getting back to court, but it was worth it—not just eating a delicacy, but in the friends I made by doing so.

I've met judges who kept themselves distant not only from the community but also from the rest of the court party. One judge treated the kitchen area attached to the band office boardroom where court was being held as his private chambers and he retired there during breaks to avoid conversations. I know there was no chair in the kitchen, so for the better part of an hour he either remained standing or lay down on the floor or on the counter, while next door counsel negotiated and interviewed witnesses. I suppose the prestige of his position demanded that he make such sacrifices. Another judge, who was appointed just when the local courthouse was being renovated, insisted that the carpet in the judge's offices be of a better quality than the carpet in the clerical area. Maintenance people snickered at his arrogance, but complied. Judges' arrogance was not confined to their choice of carpet or to where they rested; they brought this same attitude into the courtroom.

But the most common reason I was given for the reluctance of witnesses to come forward was that they were afraid of how they would be treated if they were implicated in sending someone to jail. When you live in a Far North community, your survival depends on that community. Basic groceries in stores are prohibitively expensive. Most people cannot afford to buy meat, and they rely on hunters to provide for the community. In the Far North, caribou are a staple. I once spoke with a woman who told me her family of five survived on ten caribou a year. She is lucky. Her husband is a hunter and owns a snow-mobile. With declining caribou populations, hunters have to travel farther and farther every year. In 2019, it was a twelve-hour snowmobile drive to get to where the caribou were. Being a hunter and owning a snow machine meant her husband also had an obligation to provide for the community.

Sharing is fundamental. Once, I was out front of the community hall in Black Lake chatting with a few people during a court break. I was asking about the caribou hunt. It was early in the season and I wanted to know how far away they were. How many were there? What were conditions like reaching them? I was told that one person had managed to get out and bring back some caribou. I was told the person's name, and a woman pointed out his house. "The orange-and-white one over there. If you want meat, just go and knock. He will give you some." I am certain that if I had walked to that house, knocked on the door and asked for caribou meat, the hunter would have shared, even though he didn't know me. Such is our culture.

Meat is the most fundamental example of our sharing, but it extends to everything. Indigenous Peoples are the people who share. We share our meat, our fish, our firewood, our money, our childcare, our elder care, and our alcohol.

Now imagine testifying in a foreign court against a community member who then gets sent away to jail. How would you go to a close relative of that person to ask for meat? Or to another to ask for childcare? Because we tend to be closely related in our small communities, the person you testified against is likely to be your relative as well. His mother is your auntie. You share a grandmother. His sister works in the same place as you. Now you have to face all these people who all know that it's because of you that he has been sent away.

When I talked to people hesitant to testify, they did not mention that meat might not be shared or that favours would be withheld, but they were afraid of what might be said to them and how they might be treated. They knew that if they asked for meat it would probably be shared with them. They wouldn't get the choicest cut, but they would get something. The person sharing might toss it to them, like throwing to a dog.

These reluctant witnesses were most afraid of what their auntie or their grandmother might say. Imagine going to the local store or a community event and meeting someone who speaks loudly and harshly to you because someone close to them was recently sent to jail and you had testified on behalf of the Crown.

Then imagine everyone near enough to hear the harsh words looking downward or away.

It works both ways. Indigenous people don't want to be part of the court process, and those involved in the court process do not want to actively engage the community. When I was a part of that process I, too, had to accept things as they had always been done—that we would hold ourselves above the people, maintaining our position of prestige and privilege, our superiority and our authority.

8

When white people appear in court,
they are treated differently.

FLAT EARTHERS, CLIMATE change deniers and
people who promote the idea that race doesn't matter
all refuse to look at the evidence. Ask any brown-
skinned person if race matters and they will provide all
the evidence necessary. Race is often the single most
important aspect of a person's identity. If you are other
than white and you live in a territory dominated by
whites, the simple reality is that your race will largely
determine most things about your lived experience.

Race is so fundamental to our existence that the
refusal of the justice system to consider it means that
system has closed its mind to our reality. Justice
prides itself on its blindness, taking as its emblem the

blindfolded woman with a scale in one hand and a sword in the other. But how can it judge me if it refuses to look at me, and if it looks at me, refuses to see the essential of who I am? We often speak of systemic racism. It's not the system that's racist. It's the participants. It's the judge and the prosecutor and the defence counsel and the clerk and the police officer and the prison guard and the accused and the victim. We are all racist, and we are not going to fix anything if we keep denying it.

When white people appear in court, they are treated differently.[5] I witnessed it throughout my time as a practising lawyer. The judge is usually white, the prosecutor is usually white, the defence counsel is usually white. When the accused looks and sounds like the judge and the prosecutor and defence counsel, it is more likely he will be believed. And the defence counsel and the prosecutor and the judge do not take that necessary moment to confront their own racism before they make arrangements that are to the benefit of the accused. Not only is he more likely to be believed, but he is more likely to be sentenced more leniently and the conditions placed upon him will be the least restrictive given the level of his offence.

The *Annual Report of the Office of the Correctional Investigator 2016-2017* states that between 2007 and 2016, while the overall federal prison population increased by less than 5 percent, the Indigenous prison population increased by 39 percent and the number of Caucasian offenders decreased by 14.7 percent over the same period.

I have had many conversations with members of the legal profession about discrimination against Indigenous Peoples. The vast majority of these people claim to treat everyone the same. But, as broad as those discussions have been, I have not heard anything said about favouritism toward their own.

Close to the end of my career as a Crown prosecutor, I had a file involving a seventeen-year-old white male charged with an assault on his parents and placed on conditions to abstain from possessing or consuming alcohol, to abide by a curfew and to keep the peace. This young man continuously breached his conditions, and eventually I asked the judge to keep him in remand until his trial. The judge refused. Okay, I thought, so the judge is giving the kid a break. No big deal. Sometimes people get a break.

When the police were next called to the young man's house, they found holes punched in the walls, and they came to believe that he was deliberately tormenting his parents. He was flagrantly consuming alcohol and ignored his curfew. Again I asked the judge to remand him. Again the judge refused.

I knew this judge. I did not consider him to be a racist. He took pride in his fairness toward Indigenous people. His sentencing regime was reasonably lenient. I had spent years in front of him, making the exact same arguments I was making now, only in all those other cases the youths in question had been Indigenous, and in every single one of those cases the offenders had been remanded.

At first I doubted myself. Maybe that judge refused to remand this white youth because his parents always accompanied him to court. I knew that parental involvement went a long way with this judge. But I had also known him to send Indigenous youths to jail even when their parents or grandparents were in the courtroom.

But maybe it was me being racist. Maybe I didn't like this youth because he was a settler. Was I being extra hard on him because of his race? I took the file to a couple of other prosecutors who worked in the La Ronge office. They each confirmed that, yes, in their experience anyone in the circumstances of this accused, who breached court-ordered conditions as frequently as he had, should expect to be remanded until their trial. It wasn't me. It was the judge.

The only explanation I could come up with was that to this judge, the accused looked and sounded like him. The accused's parents looked and sounded like this judge's parents. The judge probably told himself that he was simply being fair. I doubt that he ever consciously considered his own racial bias toward one of his own.

I have had many discussions about the need to change the colour of people involved in the justice system. But changing the colour of the prosecution, the judge or the jury is not going to make the situation any better. Shortly after I became a prosecutor, I had a jury trial. A young man from a northern community was charged with aggravated assault. He and his uncle had gone to the local pool hall, where a group were playing cards. They came in with a baseball bat and attacked people. No reason was ever given. We can assume it was over a past grudge. The victim ended up with a broken arm. The uncle entered a guilty plea and was sentenced. The accused denied he was there and said it must have been someone else. We were going to trial to prove identity.

I wanted an Indigenous jury because I believed that Indigenous people were more likely to understand the dynamics of small, isolated communities and the role that bullies play in those communities. I had experienced juries made up of settler people and believed that quite often they just didn't get it. Or they simply didn't care enough to try. I wanted a jury with personal experience with random violence. I wanted a jury who understood the accused, people who had a cousin just like him. I also believed that an Indigenous jury would be more likely to convict because they would have a greater moral obligation to protect the community. They would know what was going on.

I phoned the accused's defence counsel. "Hey, buddy, why don't we load up that jury with Indigenous people. You can ensure your client gets a fair trial."

"Great idea," he responded. "But I'm not sure I can tell who is Indigenous or not on the jury list."

"That's okay, I'll help. I know all the Indigenous surnames on that list."

So we loaded up that jury with Indigenous people based upon their skin colour, and if we couldn't tell by their skin colour, we selected based upon whether their surname was common among Indigenous people in the area. My friend still thinks I set him up. I swear I didn't.

It wasn't until after the jury was selected, and after I presented the Crown's case and sat back and observed the twelve men and women of the jury, when the accused took the stand in his own defence and I realized that young Dene man didn't stand a chance in front of that all-Cree jury.

Hostilities between Cree and Dene go back to the fur trade era, when Cree traders sought to exclude the Dene from access to the trading posts around Hudson

Bay. Our languages are as different as English is from Finnish. Our cultures and traditions are very different. The Dene live north of us and are caribou hunters. The Woods Cree depend more on fish and moose. Outright hostility ended a century ago, but the prejudice lingers.

I have no way of knowing whether the jury my friend and I selected convicted the accused based upon intertribal prejudice. All I know is that they weren't in the jury room for very long before they came back with a guilty verdict.

If, as is being contemplated, we change the rules around jury selection to ensure more participation by Indigenous people, we will have to pay attention to which First Nation the accused is from and which First Nations the jury are selected from. Indigenous people residing within the territory now called Canada are not homogeneous. We are multiple nations, each with different cultures, different traditions, different ceremonies, different concepts of peace and good order. We have histories with each other. The Haudenosaunee and Anishinaabe, the Dene and Inuit, the Cree and the Blackfoot all have ancient rivalries that have not been completely forgotten or forgiven. Sometimes the prejudice has a life of its own and continues long after people have forgotten the original reason.

Simply changing the colour of the people in the courtroom is not going to make a difference in the incarceration rates of Indigenous people. Many of us have had our culture educated out of us. Our political views are as diverse as those in the dominant culture. We have people who would cut down the last tree to make a dollar and people who still understand that trees are our relatives. We have people who follow a native spiritual path, but many more are fundamentalist Christians who believe fervently in punishment.

In short, there are no typical Indigenous people. We are engineers, doctors, nurses, trappers, architects, fishermen, lawyers, loggers, judges, miners, professors, teachers, social workers, police officers, bootleggers, accountants, entrepreneurs, business owners, truck drivers, bankers, tradespersons, waiters and welfare recipients. We are filmmakers and novelists and dancers and painters. We perform operas and hip hop and powwow. Our political views represent the far right and the far left and everything in between. We have Elders who are esteemed knowledge keepers and old people who have had all their traditional culture erased by residential school. We have people who know all the ceremonies and protocols and strictly follow the way they were taught by previous knowledge keepers and we have people who are just making it up as they go along.

When we select a jury, we are selecting from this vast, diverse pool. An Indigenous person tried by a jury comprising Indigenous people cannot predict a favourable outcome based solely upon a shared race. Changing the jury selection process to change the skin colour of the participants is not going to make trials more fair or reduce the over-incarceration of Indigenous people.

9

Incarceration is contagious and in many of our communities it is epidemic.

THE OVER-INCARCERATION OF Indigenous people began in earnest in about 1960 and since then has climbed steadily. The trend continues upwards despite all attempts at finding a solution. Nothing the government or the courts do makes any difference.

Indigenous people keep saying, "When you are in Indian country you have to do things differently." But we keep implementing the same policies that don't work.

Canada's administration of justice relies heavily upon the principle of deterrence, the idea, first, that if you punish someone severely enough they won't commit the same offence again and, second, that people seeing this person being punished will likely avoid the same crime themselves. As I've shown earlier, alcohol use has a close correlation with criminal activity. Intoxicated people generally do not think about the consequences of their actions. Yet the principle of deterrence relies upon the idea that people *do* think about the consequences of their actions before they commit an offence. But most people do not. They more often *re*act than act. The most common forms of violence are not planned. The fight simply happens and someone gets hurt or killed.

Despite claims that Canadian courts rely only upon proven evidence, rigorously tested at trial under strict rules to determine what might or might not be admissible, there is no evidence at all that deterrence as used by the courts has any value. In fact all the evidence shows that this type deterrence does not work. The Solicitor General of Canada commissioned a study in 2002 on the effects of prison sentences and intermediate sanctions on recidivism. The authors looked at 111 studies involving 442,000 offenders and concluded that the longer the prison sentence, the more likely the person would reoffend.[6]

Deterrence is a belief system, by which I mean that people believe it works. Showing someone evidence contrary to their belief will rarely dislodge it because believing in something does not require proof; it is simply a matter of faith. The particular belief in deterrence is peculiar to settler society and probably has roots in a Judeo-Christian religion that believes in hell-fire punishment for sins.

Incarceration is contagious and in many of our communities it is epidemic. The more we rely upon incarceration, the more we are forced to incarcerate. A criminal record doesn't matter. Most Indigenous people have one. In my experience it was so rare to find someone without a criminal record that if a twenty-five-year-old male came to court without one, it was seen as an exceptional circumstance. As a prosecutor, I handled about fifteen hundred files a year. Each of those files contained multiple charges. Multiply my fifteen hundred files by the eleven prosecutors assigned to northern Saskatchewan and you have 16,500 files a year, each containing multiple charges. The Criminal Code allows that several charges can be laid for a single incident. So, if an intoxicated person pushes a chair into another person and causes a bruise, they can be charged with assault, assault with a weapon, assault causing bodily harm, public intoxication, and mischief if they didn't own the chair and it was damaged. Then consider that only thirty-eight thousand people live here. It doesn't take very many years before most people in the territory have multiple charges on their criminal record.

The harder the courts work—the more charges we process, the more convictions we obtain the more often we rely upon incarceration—the more normal criminal records and jail time become. The administration of justice is making things worse instead of better.

Joey lives in a northern community. Drinking happens there, but it is not a constant, it is not an everyday occurrence. The stereotype of the lazy drunken Indian is simply false. In fact there are, per capita, more Indigenous people in Canada who are completely abstinent than there are among the non-Indigenous population. Thirty-five percent of Indigenous people in Canada do not use alcohol at all, compared with only 18 percent of Canadians. Most Indigenous people are sober most of the time.

Joey knows and is related to most of the people in his community. He knows his uncle is a good guy when he is sober. He takes care of his family. He is fun to be around and likes to laugh and tease. But his uncle was arrested and went to jail for something he did when he was drinking. So Joey knows that even good guys can go to jail. He knows this because not only his uncle but his father and two of his brothers have gone to jail and he knows that they are all good men when they are sober. When his uncle and his father and his brothers came back from jail they told Joey about their experiences. Joey thinks jail is not that bad a place. It might be strange and different and lonely, but people do survive and come home after. There is little stigma to jail when you see that even good guys can be sent there. A foreign colonial court doesn't have persuasive power. It simply doesn't matter what the judge and the prosecutor and the legal aid lawyer who fly in once or twice a month think. The court party's opinion is meaningless. Life in the community is going to continue the same the day after court as it did the day before court. The community doesn't necessarily look down on people because they have been to jail. They return to their families and their homes and are accepted back again.

When most of the people that Joey knows have criminal records and many of his friends and family have gone to jail, he doesn't feel any shame when it's his turn to appear in court.

As a prosecutor, I was told several times by accused people that it didn't matter whether I recommended jail or not. Jail was simply not that big a deal. I remember once informing a man that I was seeking custody for his offence, and he asked me what good I thought it would do to send him away. I didn't have an answer. These were serious conversations. These men were not blustering, they weren't acting tough or being argumentative. They were respectfully trying to educate me on the reality of their situation. They would go to jail and come back and nothing good would come of it.

Our misguided over-reliance upon incarceration is especially apparent when we sentence people suffering from FASD or other mental health problems. We in the administration of law have not found a humane way of dealing with people who have mental health issues. When we sentence them, we don't take into account their special needs. I've heard defence counsel make submissions that their client would be abused in a correctional centre and heard the judge bluntly reply that was none of his business. It was a matter for Correctional Services to address.

After a judge passes sentence, the law declares their decision functus. There is nothing more the judge can do. The matter cannot be brought back to them. Any change in the sentence has to be made through appeal. It's not just the court case that we wipe our hands of; it's everything about the offender. We write "Closed" on the file and tell ourselves the rest is someone else's responsibility.

The colloquial definition of insanity commonly but mistakenly attributed to Albert Einstein is "doing the same thing over and over again expecting a different result." The administrators of law push those boundaries further. We do things over and over knowing we are making things worse while we tell ourselves we are making things better. We really have to wonder who is more insane, the offender with an injured brain or the administrators of law. I include myself in this. I too recommended jail sentences for people I knew to be mentally ill. I told myself I was doing the job of a prosecutor and that it was up to the offender's counsel to present arguments for alternatives to jail. The problem was, of course, there rarely were alternatives. Judges frequently agreed with my submissions and sentenced the accused to incarceration. I believe they felt they had no choice.

Residential schools were dedicated to the eradication of Indigenous culture. To an extent they were successful, but merely erasing a culture didn't finish the process. A new culture was needed to replace the one that was erased. Jails accomplish this. We send people out of the community to correctional centres and penitentiaries, and they learn quickly to depend upon the institution. There is no need to work, and everything they need for shelter and sustenance is provided. They learn not to be responsible. They have no power to change their circumstances, so anything that happens to them is beyond their control. Jail is not just the removal of a person from greater society; it is also the removal of their power of choice.

Further, prisoners learn to distrust authority. There is a distinct line between the guards and prisoners. Guards are trained to never, ever become friends with a prisoner. This is rule number one for all prison guards. The fear is that prisoners will manipulate any friendship to their favour, and horror stories are told of the guard who accepted a gift and was then black-mailed into bringing drugs into the institution. Add to this the culture of power in the institutions and the documented abuses of that power by prison officials.[7] A distinct us-and-them mindset prevails on the part of both prisoners and guards. The guards teach the prisoners to disrespect them by refusing any attempt at human-to-human contact, and the prisoners re-inforce the guards' beliefs by abiding by the rule. The most despicable person in jailhouse culture is the rat. Giving information to the authorities can result in a beating or even death. For ten years, my wife worked for Correctional Services Canada in Kingston. She assures me there was a distinct "us versus them" culture prevalent across the service.

Prisoners learn that violence solves problems. When a dispute arises between prisoners, they cannot rely on the guards or the institution to resolve it. It's up to them, and violence being the main reason for incarceration for many of them, violence is resorted to in prison as well. In an environment where violence becomes natural, normal and necessary, the tough guy, the enforcer, is looked to as the leader. People sent to prison quickly learn that the tough guy is an envious role and attempt to emulate it.

Jailhouse culture also teaches that even the slightest insult must be dealt with immediately, and if necessary with violence. If another inmate says something offensive to you, he must be put in his place or he will think you are weak and next time the attack will be with more than words. The most offensive thing a person can be called in jail is a goof. In the Canadian prison system, "goof" is applied to informers, child molesters, child killers and people in protective custody, but not exclusively. It can be used more generally for anyone outside the norm. Calling someone a goof is an open invitation to a fight. If you are called a goof and do not respond immediately with violence, you are a coward and your status within the institution is diminished. You become one of the low-ranking nothings, and anyone can abuse you with impunity. Cree culture used to be a culture of teasing, but we cannot tease anymore. Now, if you say the wrong thing to the wrong person, you can get yourself stabbed.

These new cultural beliefs—that the institution will feed and shelter you, that you are not responsible, that authority can be disrespected but don't be a rat, that violence solves problems, that one must retaliate immediately to any perceived insult and that the tough guy always wins—are carried back to communities by former inmates when they are released. They come back expecting to be fed and housed. When they don't immediately get what they want, they bad-mouth the Chief and the council and the housing board. They strut around the community in a gangster swagger, intimidating people with their toughness, responding with violence to the slightest perceived insult, and they tell stories about the glory they earned in jail. I have seen a man wearing leg irons, handcuffs and a waist restraint manage to pull off a gangster swagger as he walked across the courtroom, from the prisoner's dock to the witness stand in front of the jury. He seemed quite proud of his status as a prisoner. I don't think he impressed the jury, though. They convicted him after a very short deliberation.

This jailhouse culture infects our communities, resulting in increased dependence, hopelessness and violence, and the infection results in more charges being laid, more need for police and courts and more people being sent to jail, adding another spiral to the cycle. Many Indigenous youths who have never experienced our traditional culture now believe that jailhouse culture is our culture. It has become normal. Canada's over-reliance on incarceration has made the situation of Indigenous Peoples in this country worse. Peace and good order in our communities has become merely a faint hope.

Jails are like cults, and to undo their psychological effects we need deprogrammers. We need a lot of deprogrammers to reintegrate offenders upon their release from custody. Ideally these deprogrammers would take people out into the forest because they are not yet fit to return to the community. There we would reintroduce them to their families, teach them that kindness is not weakness, teach them to make choices and own the consequences, and thus begin the process of healing not just the trauma that likely caused them to commit the offence they went to jail for to begin with, but also the trauma of committing a crime and the trauma of incarceration.

DEATH OF A BROTHER

I SPOKE ABOUT GARRY,
ABOUT HIS LIFE AND WHO HE WAS.

I have stood before a judge in a courtroom as defence counsel and as prosecutor; I have also been there to speak to the impact of a crime.

I have had two brothers killed by drunk drivers. The first was my older brother Clifford. He was on the road with his three sons when a drunk driver drove into his truck and killed him. In 2018, I published a book about Clifford.

The second brother, Garry, was run down while he was walking home one night in 2014. Hillary Cook had left a local bar late at night and swerved off the road. Garry lived for only a few minutes after being hit.

Hillary did not have a criminal record. He was well liked in the community of La Ronge. He was known for helping others. His earliest years were spent on the trapline and his first year of school was in Stanley Mission. He then spent eleven years in residential school. He was educated and worked at Kitsaki Development Corporation for over a decade, where he mostly wrote business proposals. He had served as a councillor for the Lac La Ronge Indian Band from 2005 until 2008. He made an unsuccessful run for the position of Chief in 2014. He campaigned on a platform that to address power imbalances with the federal government, members of the band council led by the Chief needed to act more like politicians and less like social workers. He wasn't known to drink excessively. Hillary had lost his wife six months before killing Garry. He was filled with grief.

The evidence presented in court showed that on the night he killed Garry, he had gone out to a neighbour's house party where he became intoxicated. He then walked home, got into his truck and drove to a bar where he was served more alcohol. When the bar closed, he headed home. He had no intention of hurting anyone. His only intention was to drink enough alcohol to numb his pain.

Garry was walking home late at night. His daughter had asked him to babysit while she went to bingo.

When she came home, she offered to hire a taxi for her father. My brother was a bushman. He was an exceptional trapper. He never owned a snow machine and worked his trapline by walking. To him, it was a waste of money to hire a taxi. He only lived about two kilometres away, a very short distance for a man who could walk in excess of thirty kilometres a day carrying a packsack through deep snow.

Garry had been in a long-term relationship that resulted in five children before it ended. His ex-partner entered into two more relationships and had two more children. Because relationships never really end and once established will continue in one form or another, Garry, his ex-partner, their children—now adults with their own kids—and his ex-partner's other two children all lived in an extended entanglement.

One of the children of the ex-partner is Brennan. Brennan's functioning is impacted by his mother's use of alcohol before he was born. He has the facial and skull features and the behavioural symptoms—poor impulse control and difficulty determining consequences—of fetal alcohol spectrum disorder, or FASD. As a child he was very difficult to manage. The only person who could handle him turned out to be Garry, and the two formed a close bond. So close that Brennan's mother left him in Garry's care.

Garry and Brennan lived with Garry's oldest daughter, Patricia, in a small, crowded house on the reserve along with Patricia's partner and their children and her two younger sisters, who also had small children, and her half-sister, who was younger than Brennan. Garry may have been the father or grandfather to most of the people in the house, but Patricia was the matriarch. It was her house, her rules, and she kept order through sheer will and determination. But Patricia could not handle Brennan. She needed Garry for that.

And then Garry was dead. And there was no one to look out for Brennan.

Hillary was charged with impaired driving causing death. He pleaded guilty.

I was too well known in the court, and neither of the local judges felt comfortable sentencing the man who had killed my brother. For the appearance of justice, an outside judge and an outside prosecutor were brought in for the sentencing hearing.

I spoke at that hearing. The law allows persons injured by crime to give victim impact statements. I was not a victim, and to me the word "victim" is derogatory. It implies powerlessness. I spoke on behalf of Garry's family. I spoke because Patricia is not a comfortable public speaker. I spoke for her brothers and sisters and their children. I spoke for Brennan. None of these people are victims. None of them are powerless.

I spoke about Garry, about his life and who he was. I wanted the court to know him. I wanted Patricia and Brennan and all of Garry's children and grand-children who filled the court that morning to know that their father and grandfather would be understood by the court.

I did not speak of revenge or retaliation because that is not what I wanted and I knew it was not what Garry's children and grandchildren wanted.

I told the presiding judge that I did not need Hillary to go to jail, that I felt no animosity toward him. But in the end he was sentenced to three years' imprisonment.

With the passing of sentence, Garry did not come back. His children were not relieved of their grief, his grandchildren did not receive a future with a man who could teach them his bush skills, and Brennan did not get someone to look out for him. The big empty space caused by Garry's passing was not filled for any of us. Three years in jail and the conclusion of a court process did not resolve any of the real things we were feeling.

The sentence did not help Hillary, either. It did not relieve him of his grief at his wife's passing. It did not relieve him of his remorse for taking a life. He had a thirteen-year-old granddaughter living with him.

Within a short time, that young girl lost her home and her grandmother, and her grandfather was sentenced to three years in prison. Her condition was not considered by the sentencing judge. She was just collateral damage. She had gone to live with Hillary because one of her young friends had hanged herself. La Ronge knows about suicide pacts and has experienced epidemics of suicide. There was no evidence the granddaughter was involved in a pact, but everyone was concerned about her.

Three years in prison did no one any good. Most people would agree that Hillary should pay a price for what he did. But we could have fashioned a sentence that did not cause more harm. Hillary should have been required to stay home, to look after his granddaughter, so that she did not end up before a different sentencing judge when she acted out because of her grief and abandonment.

While I was writing this book, I asked Hillary if he would talk to me. He agreed. I picked him up at his house on the reserve. He lives in a beautiful spot with a view right across Lac la Ronge. We went to a local restaurant that was quiet in the afternoon. I had shared a draft of what I had written about him, and he had emailed a response clarifying information that I had wrong.

He has no memory of hitting Garry. His last clear memory of that evening is walking on a trail from his neighbour's house to his own. The rest is blank. Faced with the accusation that he drove his truck and killed Garry, Hillary had no defence. There was damage to the front of his vehicle, Garry's DNA was on the front of his truck, there was video of him at the bar and video of a truck as it struck Garry captured by the surveillance camera at a roadside motel.

But Hillary knows himself. He knows he is a good person who would never harm another, let alone take a life. He recounted to me a time when he had gone for a walk along the lakeshore and encountered two men beating up a third. He knows that if he had not intervened when he did, the young man might have been murdered. One of the men was about to hit him in the head with a large rock.

Despite his guilty plea, despite taking responsibility, he is still nagged by the thought, "What if it wasn't me?" He has compiled a list of circumstantial evidence: He was with a woman that night and doesn't know what became of her. She gave a statement to the police that had inconsistencies within it. She said they had gone back to Hillary's to continue drinking, and none of the alcohol in his house had been drunk. His uncle who lives nearby heard his vehicle return home and also heard a woman screaming. There were rumours of two women in a red car that stopped and one of them was heard to say, "Oh my god, we've killed him." While there is not enough in these rumours or suspicions to establish a credible defence, they do work on his mind.

Despite these doubts about his conviction, despite his worry that the justice system might not have acted with complete fairness, at the end of the day, Hillary wants to take responsibility. He wants to make things better. He wants his family, his community and his First Nation to become better. He could imagine going into schools to speak to children who are just beginning to drink. He estimated that age to be ten or eleven, but wasn't surprised when I told him that recent school surveys indicated the age of experimentation in some places to be as young as eight.

We discussed his time in custody. Hillary said he had heard that jail was the new residential school, but in his experience residential school was much worse. In jail, if you keep to yourself and don't bother anyone, you are pretty much left alone. In residential school, if someone you happened to be beside did something wrong, you and everyone nearby were punished as well.

Hillary spent time at the Saskatchewan Penitentiary, in Prince Albert, before he was transferred to a healing lodge. At the healing lodge he encountered Elders, sweats and ceremonies. During our conversation at the restaurant, he commented upon what seemed like an over-emphasis on the weight room in prison as a recreational facility: "Why do they provide equipment to dangerous people that makes them even more dangerous?" When I asked him about the people he met in prison, Hillary said that 90 percent of them were there for something they did while they were intoxicated by alcohol or drugs and that most of them were Indigenous.

Hillary could have been ordered to look after Brennan, to take Brennan out and teach him the skills Garry never finished passing down, to help Brennan through his abandonment.

Maybe if the court had made that order, Brennan would not have ended up in jail.

When Brennan was very small he loved nothing better than to pound nails with a hammer. He was capable of figuring out anything mechanical and was renowned for keeping bicycles operational. When he was a teenager he helped me in the bush and impressed me with his ability and his willingness to work hard.

Now he is in jail. With FASD, he responds well to structure. In jail everything is organized for him. Meals are served according to a predictable schedule. Lights are turned off and on at precise times. Brennan does well in this type of environment. He doesn't do well in disorganization. He cannot navigate his way through it.

Brennan's injury affects his ability to understand consequences. He is impulsive. Put an idea into his head or challenge him to do something, and he is likely to attempt whatever is before him without thinking about the results. He is the perfect recruit for a street gang. If he is told to do something, he will likely try. He wants to please people, and once he is recruited, the gang will become his people.

We could design facilities and programs for FASD people that fulfill the requirements of routine and provide a sense of belonging. We don't. Instead we wait until they have committed an offence, and then we incarcerate them. Once they have learned jailhouse culture—and FASD people learn it very quickly—they tend to continue to offend and receive longer and longer sentences until they are declared dangerous offenders and are incarcerated indefinitely.

Brennan survives better in jail than he does in the community. That is not a recommendation for jail. It is a condemnation of our society. The services Brennan receives are directly proportional to the amount we invest, and we invest a lot more resources into correctional facilities than we do into community programs.

Brennan has ended up in the place we designed for him. It is the result we should expect.

There was only one person in the world who could give Brennan the constancy of love and care he needed, and that was Garry. Garry died because there were no supports for Hillary as he was navigating his way through his grief. We know we could reduce crime by employing more trauma counsellors and mental health and addiction workers. But we prefer to spend more on police, prosecutors and prisons. We had no issue with the added expense of bringing in an outside prosecutor and an outside judge to ensure the appearance of fairness at Hillary's sentencing hearing. We have no problem spending money on the facade of the justice system. But we struggle to find resources for communities in real need.

CLOSING ARGUMENT

THE CASE FOR INDIGENOUS JUSTICE

To reduce crime, violence and the over-incarceration of Indigenous Peoples requires an evidence-based approach. Prior to contact, First Nations administered our own laws, and all the evidence suggests we were quite successful at it. In my own Cree territory we had a police force—Semaganisak—who were specially trained and respected. There were border skirmishes with other First Nations, and sometimes one of our own acted inappropriately, but for the most part we had peace and good order.

When we entered into treaty with the Queen, we did not give up our jurisdiction over criminal law. Here is the final clause in Treaty 6, negotiated and agreed to between the Cree and Her Majesty the Queen in 1876.

> And the undersigned Chiefs on their own behalf and on behalf of all other Indians inhabiting the tract within ceded, do hereby solemnly promise and engage to strictly observe this treaty, and also to conduct and behave themselves as good and loyal subjects of Her Majesty the Queen.
>
> They promise and engage that they will in all respects obey and abide by the law, and they will maintain peace and good order between each other, and also between themselves and other tribes of Indians, and between themselves and others of Her Majesty's subjects, whether Indians or whites, now inhabiting or hereafter to inhabit any part of the said ceded tracts, and that they will not molest the person or property of any inhabitant of such ceded tracts, or the property of Her Majesty the Queen, or interfere with or trouble any person passing or travelling through the said tracts, or any part thereof, and that they will aid and assist the officers of Her Majesty in bringing to justice and punishment any Indian offending against the stipulations of this treaty, or infringing the laws in force in the country so ceded.

This concluding clause of Treaty 6 retained our jurisdiction over justice in our territory. We had always maintained peace and good order amongst ourselves. The text of the treaty merely recognized our authority to continue to do so. The promise to obey and abide by the law was a promise to obey the laws in force at the time, which were our own laws.

The choice of words is significant. The phrase "peace and good order" held a distinct meaning at the time of treaty negotiations. The British North America Act of 1867, passed nine years before Treaty 6, granted to the new Dominion of Canada power over "Peace, Order, and good Government." The phrase has roots going back to the Royal Proclamation of 1763, in which King George III granted power to the new colonies over "Peace, Welfare, and good Government." It is repeated in the Quebec Act (1774), the Constitutional Act (1791) that created Upper and Lower Canada, and again in the Act of Union (1840), which united the two provinces into the Province of Canada. When the Queen's representative drafted Treaty 6, he chose to use words with distinct constitutional meaning. We not only retained jurisdiction to maintain peace and good order amongst ourselves; the treaty went further than that and granted the power to maintain peace and good order between ourselves and other tribes of

Indians, and between ourselves and others of Her Majesty's subjects, whether Indians or whites, then inhabiting or thereafter to inhabit any part of the said ceded tracts.

First Nation Peoples of Treaty 6 Territory are recognized as having jurisdiction in the British North America Act of 1867 and had that jurisdiction extended by the Queen in 1876. The Dominion of Canada and First Nation Peoples are recognized by the Crown as having equal jurisdiction over law-making and law enforcement. The Constitution of Canada does not override Treaty 6; we both get our law-making power from the same source.

The final treaty clause stipulates that we "will aid and assist the officers of Her Majesty." That doesn't necessarily mean officers of Canada's North-West Mounted Police or Canada's Royal Canadian Mounted Police. Those are officers of Her Majesty, but a police force established by us would also be officers of Her Majesty. Peace officers in Canada, as defined in the Criminal Code, may be mayors, reeves, conservation officers, fisheries officers, border guards, prison guards, police officers, immigration officers, airplane pilots, or members of the Canadian Armed Forces. As peace officers, they are all officers of Her Majesty.

Any peacekeeping force that we establish would

also be officers of Her Majesty. If a mayor or reeve can be an officer of Her Majesty, so can a Chief or band councillor. If we retake our jurisdiction over law enforcement or the environment or border security, or establish detention centres, then we can designate those employees as also being officers of Her Majesty.

The treaties with the Queen did not give Canada jurisdiction over us. The treaties gave Canada the right to exist. Canada did not gain jurisdiction through discovery. Discovery bestows no rights in international law. The Australians and Afrikaners claimed rights through *terra nullius*, or no one's land, based upon the premise that when the settlers arrived there were no humans there. The Australian High Court decision Mabo v. Queensland (No.2) (1992) put an end to *terra nullius*. The United States claims to have conquered the territory it took from the original inhabitants despite international law that denies conquest as a legitimate source of jurisdiction. The Supreme Court of Canada has stated that we were never conquered, and so Canada cannot rely upon discovery, empty land or conquest as the source of its jurisdiction. Treaty is the only legitimate source through which Canada received jurisdiction. Our treaties are foundational documents equivalent to the Constitution.

It is a fundamental principle of Canadian law that

the honour of the Crown must be upheld in all matters. The Crown cannot be seen to be involved in sharp
dealing, yet court decisions about Canadian sover-
eignty continue to be premised upon the idea that the
Crown asserted jurisdiction over all of Canada. The
Crown's assertion of jurisdiction puts it in an unten-
able situation. Without a valid justification for its sov-
ereignty, it appears that when the Crown asserted its
jurisdiction over all of Canada, in effect it stole the
land without a legal or moral basis. This proposition
puts the honour of the Crown in jeopardy.

The Dominion of Canada usurped our law-making
and law-enforcement jurisdiction when it sent the
North-West Mounted Police into our territory in
1885 and began to arrest and hang people. That portion of the treaty that says "they will not molest the
person or property of any inhabitant of such ceded
tracts, or the property of Her Majesty the Queen, or
interfere with or trouble any person passing or trav-
elling through the said tracts, or any part thereof"
simply implies that when we administer justice in
our territories, we will do so in a fair fashion. It ties
in with the previous clause in which we promise to
be good and loyal subjects of the Queen, the same
way that other Canadians are expected to be her
good and loyal subjects. Both First Nations and

Canada are expected to administer justice in their respective territories fairly.

If the Dominion assumes jurisdiction over law-making and law enforcement, then it has the duty to create and enforce laws that keep peace and good order. The Dominion has failed in that duty.

The present state in many of our communities cannot be described as peaceful or orderly, and the state of affairs between ourselves and others of Her Majesty's subjects now inhabiting or hereafter to inhabit any part of the said ceded tracts is nearing a race war. Not only has the Dominion usurped our jurisdiction and imposed its own, it has done a very poor job of keeping peace and good order.

The fundamental difference between how First Nations would maintain peace and good order and how Canada has administered it is that First Nations would apply principles of redemption, whereas Canada relies upon deterrence. We know that punishment as deterrence does not work to reduce criminal behaviour. Punishment, no matter how severe, does not modify behaviour. The United States relies heavily upon punishment and has the highest rate of incarceration in the world, yet after several decades of being tough on crime cannot show any improvement in crime rates. The numbers vary depending upon which factors are considered, but most reports have the United States incarcerating around 700 out of every 100,000 citizens, or nearly one percent of its population. Those same reports have Canada incarcerating a little more than 100 out of every 100,000. Denmark, Sweden and Norway are reported at about 60 per 100,000 and Japan is reported to incarcerate about 40 per 100,000.

When we talk about the revolving door of the justice system we are usually referring to the perception that people are released, commit more crimes, are arrested again and brought back in. Justice is part of a revolving system, but it is more complex than this simple perception. Justice never resolves the problems it adjudicates. After the judge issues the sentence and after the prosecutor writes "Closed" on the cover of the file, nothing changes in the community. One community member might be gone for a few months or years, but they will come back, probably worse off than when they left. Other than that, the sentencing decision, no matter how severe, has not had any positive effect on the community. It has not deterred anyone from committing a similar offence. It has not reduced the crime rate. It has not addressed any of the underlying factors that result in crime.

Redemption, on the other hand, is focused on solving the problem and making things right again. When we sentenced Hillary Cook to three years in prison, we did nothing to reduce the number of people killed by drunk drivers, Garry didn't come back, his children and grandchildren were not spared their grief, Brennan did not get a mentor, and Hillary wasn't given the opportunity to make amends for his big mistake.

In all my years practising criminal law, I never met anyone I would call "criminal." A criminal is someone who deliberately behaves criminally for their own long-term benefit. I met people who drank too much and while under the influence committed violent acts up to and including atrocities. Some of these people were so unhealthy they were a danger to themselves or to others. Yet I never met anyone who consciously planned to act criminally for their own prolonged betterment. Sometimes a person would rob a liquor store or a bank, but it was always to satisfy some immediate need rather than a long-range strategy.

Long-term, repeat sexual offenders also don't meet the definition of criminal even if their actions are planned and deliberate and for their personal gratification. There is something wrong with these people. They seem to be trapped in a perverse pattern of thinking that is perhaps related to addictions. So far, we have not found any successful treatments, and jail remains the best available solution to protect people from them.

I am sure there are true criminals out there. I've just never met any.

I remember prosecuting a murder charge and being very impressed by one of the investigating officers. The work of the Major Crime Unit of the RCMP is demanding, and this officer appeared to have it all together. He was prepared, he was polite, he never overstated his case and he treated the accused decently. During a break in the trial, while we were standing in the hallway of the courthouse, he told me, "It changed when I quit thinking of us and them. It's all just us. They're the same as me. They just messed up."

The idea of the criminal gives politicians something to protect us from. The promise to be tough on crime is a good vote-garnering slogan. But longer prison sentences and more police officers and stricter sanctions do not reduce the violence in our communities. They increase it. Labelling someone a criminal does not assist in that person's rehabilitation and it limits their ability to re-engage with their community and to become a productive member of it.

Renowned epidemiologist Sir Michael Marmot has brought global attention to the social determinants of health. He has shown how wealth disparities influence longevity. The life expectancy of a person living in a rough part of a city might be as much as twenty years shorter than that of a person living in a wealthier part of the same city.[8]

We have a poverty problem in Canada, with one in five children living in poverty. In Saskatchewan it is worse, at one in four. But poverty alone is not the problem. Cuba, for example, has an average income of about $10,000 annually yet has better life expectancies than the United States, which has an average annual income four times higher. And since 2015, the life expectancy of U.S. citizens has been going down, mostly because of overdoses and suicides.

The problem seems to be about hope. People living in impoverished conditions tend to have less hope that anything will ever change. In the famous marshmallow test conducted at Stanford University in the 1970s, children were offered either one marshmallow now or two if they waited fifteen minutes. Follow-up studies showed that those who chose to wait did better in future years, with lower body mass indexes and higher SAT scores. The marshmallow test was more predictive of life outcomes than IQ tests.

What the marshmallow test shows is that people will postpone immediate gratification if they believe they will later be rewarded. People who do not believe a reward is coming, who do not have hope, will take the certainty of immediate gratification. People without hope will smoke the cigarette now knowing it will shorten their lives, will eat the cake now knowing it will affect their waistlines and their health, and will drink the alcohol now knowing it causes heart disease, stroke and cancer and will impair their decision-making, resulting sometimes in severe problems.

Crime rates are higher in impoverished areas, in these pockets of hopelessness with their shabby housing, unemployment, addictions, underfunded primary schools, scarcity of healthy food and scarcity of natural space and where predators from neighbouring communities come to buy drugs and sex. When hope has been siphoned away, all that remains is daily existence.

When you have no hope of finding a job, why bother to look for one? When you have no hope of a college or university degree, why go to high school? When today holds no more promise than yesterday, why bother to get out of bed?

When you have no hope, no promise of a future, judicial principles of deterrence have no meaning. When you commit a criminal act today to satisfy an immediate need, you are not thinking about the sentence a judge will impose upon you eighteen months in the future. You are not thinking about how that sentence will result in a criminal record and how that record will hinder your ability to find a job or keep you out of select professions.

No, today you are going to get drunk, because drunk is better than reality, and if someone pisses you off, or you are pissed at them for something they did yesterday, or you are pissed off just because, then you are going to act violently, or destructively, and the police are going to come and arrest you and the police remember you from last time so you are not going to get a break and you are going into custody. When you are released from custody you will have even less hope.

There are never easy answers to complex problems. The administration of criminal law touches on almost all aspects of our lives: education, mental health, addictions, poverty, gender relations, family, children, security, communities and nations. But changing one clause in the Criminal Code could have significant, widespread impact. If we replaced "deterrence" with "redemption," the very first act of redemption would have to be an apology for the harms committed. The offender would still pay a price, but it would be paid to the victims and the community through some form of service. Instead of looking at sentencing digests to determine the length of incarceration a particular offence required, a prosecutor would ask the community and the victims what they needed to make things right.

I predict the most profound change would be to the offender. Redemption has two parts. The first part is making the community and the victim whole again. The second part is healing the offender, or what is referred to in the Criminal Code as rehabilitation. Once the offender earned his way back into his community he would regain his pride and dignity, instead of being angry and mean. He could feel that he was contributing and making things better. And once redemption was complete, he would not have a criminal record to limit his potential.

Redemption would not be about forcing the offender to make reparations. It would be about allowing him to work his way back into his community. Redemption cannot be compelled. It must be earned. Amending the Criminal Code would take responsibility away from the administrators of law and give it to the victim, the community and the offender.

Close to the end of my interview with Hillary Cook, he mentioned that he wanted to go into schools and speak to youth about the dangers of drinking. A few days later I received an invitation from Students Against Dangerous Driving (SADD) to speak to high school students in La Ronge. I asked if I could bring

Hillary along, and they agreed. I talked about alcohol in general and what it felt like to lose a brother to an impaired driver. Hillary spoke about what it felt like to wake up in the morning, unable to remember the night before, to find damage to his truck and be told that he was responsible for a death.

Hillary and I presented to Mothers Against Drunk Driving (MADD) in Pinehouse on April 24, 2019, at the beginning of their memorial walk down the highway to the crash site where several members of that community had lost their lives. Seeing Hillary and me together helps people reconcile their grief. When I show that I can forgive the man who is responsible for my brother's death, it helps them to be more forgiving.

But, for me, the best part of of these presentations is that Hillary is earning his redemption. Three years in prison did not allow him to make amends. Going into schools and into the community and speaking honestly about what happened helps both Hillary and the community. Hillary has a long way to go to earn his way back into society, but he is working at it. If other opportunities arise for us to present together, we will accept.

Incarceration would still be a recourse for those offenders who were unwilling to accept responsibility for their actions, to apologize and work at making things right. But we would incarcerate many fewer people.

If we are serious about finding solutions to the over-incarceration of Indigenous and marginalized people, we have to look at what is working, instead of relying upon ideologies that are proven failures. We could begin by analyzing the recidivism rates of probation officers' clients. Find the top ten probation officers whose clients reoffended the least and ask them what they are doing that is different. We would probably find that they practise empathy, that they listen well and that they have a relationship with the offender. But we won't know until we ask.

When we are done with the probation officers, we could analyze the recidivism outcomes of individual prosecutors. What are they doing that is different? Then we could look at the recidivism outcomes of individual judges. Do they have any impact based upon their sentencing practices? Then we could look at the recidivism outcomes of defence counsel, beginning with legal aid. Do some jails have better outcomes than others? Which parole boards have better outcomes? Once we have the information and have analyzed it, we would have a better idea of what works and what doesn't. If we revised laws and changed policies based upon measured outcomes, we might improve those outcomes.

This evidence-based approach to solving recidivism is easily implemented and I predict would positively influence outcomes. I really don't expect either the federal or provincial departments of justice to implement these ideas. In my time in the justice system, there was a lot of talk about potential changes, but rarely were there any substantial changes. It seems the system is too large, too cumbersome, and too entrenched to ever change.

In early October of 2015, one of my prosecution points was Hatchet Lake, up in the northeastern corner of Saskatchewan. I had reached a moment when I could no longer ignore the mounting evidence that justice as I was practicing it was making things worse.

Newly appointed deputy minister of corrections Dale McFee was on the plane that day. He'd come up north with us to see what was happening on the ground. He spent the day with the probation officer, who had a table set up in the back of the band hall where we were conducting court. Throughout the day, people on probation or bail orders reported to her. At the end of the day, as we were flying from Hatchet Lake back to La Ronge, Dale said, "Forty-five people reported to probations today. Forty-four of them said they had a problem with alcohol; the forty-fifth was a twelve-year-old boy with FASD. Harold, what are we going to do?"

"Indigenous people have to change the story we tell ourselves about alcohol," I said.

"What can government do to help?" Dale asked. My big mouth answered before my brain could stop it. "Give me a six-month leave of absence and I will show you."

He gave me the leave and appointed me, my wife Joan, who was working as a special needs probation officer, and Carla Frohaug, a probation supervisor, to form the Northern Alcohol Strategy. We began our work January 1, 2016. The first thing we did was go to the Lac La Ronge Indian Band to ask the Chief and the band council to endorse our efforts. Then we went to the town of La Ronge and the village of Air Ronge to get their respective mayors and councils to endorse us too.

We wanted to create a community action plan, but we first needed to ask the people what they wanted. We tried to hold community meetings, but had to cancel several times because the hall we wanted was being used for funerals or wakes. When we were finally able to hold the meetings, most of the people who showed up were people paid to be there—social workers, addictions workers. Attending was part of their job description. We needed to hear from them, but not just them. We changed strategies and instead of asking people to come to us, we went to the people. We approached people in the courtroom who were waiting for their case to be called. We talked to business owners and the Chamber of Commerce. We interviewed people standing in line to receive a welfare cheque. I went door to door and interviewed people in their homes. We went to people's offices and asked them about alcohol and the community. We talked to clergy and pipe carriers and sweat lodge keepers. I gave the Sunday sermon at the United Church. Everywhere we went we tried to create allies.

We spoke to the local doctors the day after the La Ronge Health Centre had just experienced one of the worst weekends in their emergency department's history. They had been so busy they'd had to step over intoxicated people passed out on the floor—and some of the people there became more intoxicated because they were stealing and drinking hand sanitizer. The doctors were ready for something, *anything* that promised change. They became our greatest allies.

Dr. James Irvine, the Medical Health Officer responsible for the north, obtained permission to study alcohol and the emergency room. For the month of October 2016, the reason for every visit to emergency was documented. He then took that data and put it on a graph that he overlaid with data we collected from

the RCMP and the Saskatchewan Liquor and Gaming
Authority (SLGA). Irvine's graph showed a series of
paydays across the top: government paydays, band
paydays, and child tax credit, welfare, and old age pen-
sion days.

The graph revealed that alcohol purchases went up
in relation to the paydays, as did RCMP calls for service related to alcohol and emergency room visits
related to alcohol. We obtained school attendance
records that revealed students were more often absent
from school the day before the cheques arrived, and
that they didn't return for a few days after.

We organized a seminar with the College of
Physicians and Surgeons of Saskatchewan and brought
in experts to train our doctors, nurses, pharmacists,
social workers, addiction workers, lawyers, police officers, conservation officers, business owners, and even
Elders from neighbouring communities in evidence-
based strategies for problematic alcohol use. In one
week, over two hundred community members received
training in pharmacological interventions and trauma-
informed strategies. We brought in experts to help
teachers in both the province- and band-run schools
have honest conversations with youth about alcohol.

After a lot of work and community discussion, the
Town of La Ronge changed the local bylaw stipulating

the hours alcohol could be sold. Previously, alcohol had been sold until three a.m., though even the taxis quit running at one a.m. Under the new hours, the sale of alcohol is prohibited after eleven p.m., Monday to Saturday, with Sunday hours from one p.m. to eight p.m.

The government-run liquor store agreed to provide copies of Canada's Low-Risk Alcohol Drinking Guidelines with each purchase. Now, when the RCMP release people from the drunk tank in the morning, officers talk to them about the reason for their arrest and about their overuse of alcohol, and they provide them with information on resources available in the community to help.

These and many other activities, like the Students Against Destructive Decisions information campaign, have continued during the three years of the Northern Alcohol Strategy.

In 2019, data revealed the results of our efforts and community engagement. The crime rate in the La Ronge region is down. Calls for RCMP service went down, alcohol sales went down, and emergency room visits related to injuries decreased by fifteen per cent. An entire community came together to have an honest conversation about alcohol. The conversation was not easy. People had to examine their own use of alcohol and their style of drinking. But we have proven it can be done. Crime can be reduced simply by the community taking action. It takes local people to solve local problems.

The idea that Indigenous Peoples resume jurisdiction over criminal law in their territories is not new. The Aboriginal Justice Inquiry, commissioned in Manitoba in 1988, recommended that Aboriginal Peoples assume jurisdiction gradually, first taking over summary offences and then, when firmly established, taking over all criminal law. The commissioners recommended that the provincial government enact legislation recognizing Aboriginal jurisdiction, and that the federal government amend both the Criminal Code and the Indian Act to allow for the transference of jurisdiction. The 1996 report of the Royal Commission on Aboriginal Peoples also recommended that "federal, provincial and territorial governments recognize the right of Aboriginal nations to establish and administer their own systems of justice pursuant to their inherent right of self-government, including the power to make laws, within the Aboriginal nation's territory."

It has been more than thirty years since the establishment of the Manitoba Inquiry and nearly thirty years since Canada established the Royal Commission on Aboriginal Peoples. In those three decades the incarceration rates of Aboriginal Peoples have steadily increased. New plagues like HIV/AIDS and opiates and crystal meth have devastated our communities. Saskatchewan's AIDS infection rate is about 15 per 100,000 compared to the national average of 6 per 100,000. Pockets like the Prince Albert area have infection rates as high as 66 per 100,000 and the whole north of the province, the area where I live and work, has an infection rate of about 27 per 100,000. About 75 percent of the people with AIDS in Saskatchewan are Indigenous and the most frequent cause of infection is injection drug use, at about 67 percent of infections, followed by transmission through heterosexual sex, at about 20 percent of infections.

Our suicide rates continue to escalate, with outbreaks occurring sporadically, jumping from one community to the next. Our populations are swelling and bursting out of the reserves. Today, more than half of Indigenous people in Canada live in urban areas. For many of our people, the city experience is one of ghettoization and marginal existence.

At an Elders gathering I attended in northern Saskatchewan, a woman spoke quite forcefully and asserted that in her experience the problems in her community could be traced to two causes: the imposition of welfare and the justice system. Both had been used to destroy the community of her childhood. Those outside forces had come in and replaced all the goodness she remembered, with uncaring bureaucracies that did not have the best interests of her community in mind. They were there to serve their own purpose.

It was probably that Elder woman's words that started me thinking. I knew welfare was a destructive force, knew that intimately from personal experience. After my father died my mother had been forced to quit trapping and go on welfare. But that the justice system was destructive as well was a new idea to me then. I began to pay attention.

Now, after nearly a decade of close observation and thought, I am convinced that the justice system is making our existence worse. We can no longer wait for Canada or the provinces to make changes. They are clearly not going to come and fix this. It is not in their interest to do so. We have to do it ourselves. We have to reclaim our jurisdiction, establish our own processes. We can copy the settlers' system of courts with police and prosecutors and judges, or we can find new mechanisms that work for us. We can work in collaboration with Canada and the provinces, negotiate agreements and funding, but we do not have to ask their permission; we do not need their approval.

Whatever we do, we have to do it soon. The trajectory of increased incarceration, violence, hopelessness and death points increasingly toward our extermination. We cannot wait. Our continued existence depends upon our own action. Canada cannot wait either. There are not enough police officers or military personnel to handle what is coming. Indigenous people are primarily young—according to 2016 Canadian Census data, the average age of the Indigenous population was 32.1 years, nearly a decade younger than the non-Indigenous population at 40.9 years—and frustrated. Today we are taking out our frustrations on ourselves and on those around us, hence the suicides and violence. But we are not going to keep doing that. We will start taking out our frustrations on the colonizer. At some point we will stop killing ourselves and our relatives and begin killing the oppressor.

Canada is not going to decolonize its justice system in time. We were talking about Aboriginal Peoples and the justice system long before the Manitoba Inquiry or the Royal Commission. I have heard Ovide Mercredi talk about attending an "Indians and the Law" conference in 1970. We had interesting discussions on the subject when I was in law school almost three decades ago. I have attended conferences and symposiums across Canada over the years discussing the decolonization or indigenizing of the justice system. We have been talking for about fifty years now and not a thing has changed.

I must recommend to the participants in the justice system who are concerned about Indigenous Peoples that they cease and desist. Stop holding conferences. Stop with the symposiums. Give it up. You are wasting air. You haven't even implemented the modest tinkering that you endlessly discuss. Your ideas are too little and too late. Instead of coming together for discussions amongst yourselves, spend the time, energy and money you presently waste by having those same conversations with Indigenous Peoples. If you insist on holding a symposium, make sure you hear from someone who has spent time in your jails. If your conference is in a city, bring in Indigenous people from the street, give them something to eat, let them warm up and then listen to what they have to say. You are never going to find solutions if you continue to have conversations about us without us.

To Indigenous Peoples across Canada, I remind you, you do not need permission to create your own justice systems. You have the resources. You have Elders and knowledge keepers who remember. You have lawyers and judges and court workers. You can have police forces that work for the people instead of against the people. The transition will involve hurdles. Those who have a vested interest in the present system, whose identities and self-worth are woven into the fabric of the system, are going to oppose you. But be assured, the majority of Canadians also know the present system is not working for them, either. You will have allies.

I can hear the screaming, the gnashing of teeth, the pulling of hair—"What about the nepotism, the favouritism, the petty community feuds? What about one law for all? Equality? The Charter, damn it, the Charter!"

I have only one reply: it couldn't be any worse than what we have now.

ACKNOWLEDGEMENTS

I consulted widely in preparing this work. Thank you to the many people who participated in those discussions. There are too many to list them all, but I would like to especially recognize Gerald Morin, Claude Fafard, Stan Jolly, Rupert Ross, Sakej Henderson, Rick Bell, Neil McLeod, Gregory Lyndon, Erin Layton, Sid Robinson, Ed Stevens, Wayne Buckle, Bob Lane, Rob MacKenzie, Joan Johnson, Carla Frohaug, Ray Johnson, Harmony Johnson-Harder, Memegwans, Anangons, Wes Fineday, Eleanor Sunchild, Marlyn Poitras, Philip Charles, Jonathon Rodin, Beverly Jacobs, Sedley Brown, Hillary Cook, Vivienne Biesel, Allen Morin, Ray Desjarlais, Don Bird, Tammy Cook-Searson, David McLeod, Dale

McFee, Allen Adam, Greg Bauman, and Martha Kanya Forstner, you have all participated in the conversation and contributed to the ideas, and I thank you and at the same time claim all omissions and errors as exclusively mine.

NOTES

1   Bessel van der Kolk, *The Body Keeps the Score: Brain, Mind, and Body in the Healing of Trauma* (New York: Viking, 2014), 95.

2   *Criminal Code*, RSC 1985, c. C-46, s. 33.1:

- When defence not available

  (1) It is not a defence to an offence referred to in subsection (3) that the accused, by reason of self-induced intoxication, lacked the general intent or the voluntariness required to commit the offence, where the accused departed markedly from the standard of care as described in subsection (2).

- Criminal fault by reason of intoxication

  (2) For the purposes of this section, a person departs markedly from the standard of reasonable care generally recognized in Canadian society and is thereby criminally at fault where the person, while in a state of self-induced

intoxication that renders the person unaware of, or incapable of consciously controlling, their behaviour, voluntarily or involuntarily interferes or threatens to interfere with the bodily integrity of another person.

- Application

  (3) This section applies in respect of an offence under this Act or any other Act of Parliament that includes as an element an assault or any other interference or threat of interference by a person with the bodily integrity of another person.

3   R. v. Bouchard-Lebrun, 3 SCR 575 (2011), SCC 58 (CanLII), http://canlii.ca/t/fp2ro, retrieved on 5 April 2018.

4   Stockwell, T., Zhao, J., & Thomas, G.: *Gerald Thomas Report*.
    Centre for Addictions Research of British Columbia, University of Victoria (Received 9 October 2007; revised 11 December 2007; in final form 20 December 2007).

5   Jeff Latimer and Laura Foss, "The Sentencing of Aboriginal and Non-Aboriginal Youth under the Young Offenders Act: A Multivariate Analysis," *Canadian Journal of Criminology and Criminal Justice* 47, no. 3 (July 2005): 481–500.

6   Smith, P., Goggin, C., & Gendreau, P. (2002). The effects of prison sentences and intermediate sanctions on recidivism: General effects and individual differences (User Report 2002-01). Ottawa: Solicitor General of Canada.

7   For example, see Marion Warnica, "Edmonton

Institution Runs on 'Culture of Fear' and Intimidation, Report Finds," CBC News, June 22, 2017.

8   Michael Marmot, *The Health Gap: The Challenge of an Unequal World* (London: Bloomsbury, 2015).